THE CHILD
IN OUR HANDS
Series

PARENTING
WITH
PURPOSE

Nurturing Faith and Life
from Birth to Age Six

ODDBJØRN EVENSHAUG

DAG HALLEN

ROLAND MARTINSON

ISBN 1-889407-41-0

Published and Distributed by:

Youth & Family Institute of Augsburg College
Campus Box 70, 2211 Riverside Ave.
Minneapolis, Minnesota 55454

www.youthfamilyinstitute.com

Editors: Dr. Dick Hardel, Sonja Albers, Marilyn Sharpe

Design: by Bob Friederichsen

Photos: Mindy Bak, Vanessa Branch, Steve Friederichsen,
Lisa Haley, Carolyn Hardel, Carolyn Munson, Tom Polzine,
Mary B Reiners

TABLE OF CONTENTS

PREFACE

The Youth and Family Institute of Augsburg College is pleased to present the first of **The Child In Our Hands Series**, *Parenting With Purpose*. The authors of this book not only have wisdom and knowledge in this field of study, but it is their passion to strengthen families to nurture faith.

Before I thank God for the gifts of our authors, I must thank God for the relationship our Institute has with the Church of Norway. Much of what the Youth and Family Institute offers congregations and families was learned first from the ministry of the Church of Norway. Their National Church leaders willingly shared the strengths of their ministry to the home, called *Tripp Trapp*, and invited us to take the model further and apply it to the needs of people of the United States of America. God continues to bless us as we grow in friendship and a working partnership of the Gospel.

The major part of this book was first written by Oddbjørn Evenshaug and Dag Hallen and published in Norway as part of the Tripp Trapp ministry. The title of the book in Norwegian: **BARNET PÅ VEI MOT SELVSTENDIGHET**, translated into English is *The Child—On the Road to Independence.* From Norway the original book was translated into German, then later into Icelandic and Danish.

I met Dag Hallen and Oddbjørn Evenshaug on my first visit to Norway when Dr. David W. Anderson and I gave our first presentation of what our Institute has done with their model. The wisdom and skills of these two men is impressive. But what I felt was their greatest strength was their faith in Christ, their love of the Church, and their passion to pass on the faith from generation to generation. They told me that they worked together on every sentence of the manuscript and probably never worked harder on a manuscript. They are pleased to be able to share it with us. I thank God for them.

Another great friendship and partnership our Institute has is with Dr. Roland Martinson, professor of Pastoral Care at Luther Seminary in St. Paul, MN. He may be one of the best known and loved professors in the Evangelical Lutheran Church in America. He, too, knows Dag and Oddbjørn, and is well acquainted with the ministry of the Church of Norway. Rollie, as his many friends call him, has used his knowledge of family systems theory and written new chapters and material for this book. He also adapted the original text to the American cultural setting. He, too, has a wonderful depth of faith in Christ, a love for the Church, a passion for passing on the faith, and a willingness to share his gifts. Rollie is a Senior Associate of the Youth and Family Institute. I thank God for the friendship and work of Dr. Roland Martinson.

The Youth and Family Institute of Augsburg College has emphasized that to pass on the faith effectively from generation to generation it is best for the home and congregation to work in partnership in teaching and nurturing faith. Research clearly shows that the home is the primary place for nurturing faith. The role of the congregation, the gathered, public church, is to strengthen families to nurture the faith of the children that God has given them. Tending the baptismal journey is from cradle to the grave. The primary years for building a strong faith foundation are pre-birth to age six. This first book of **The Child In Our Hands Series**, *Parenting With Purpose* is designed for parents of children from birth through age 6.

Giving parents a copy of this book is just one way a congregation can support a family in nurturing faith. The authors made this book very practical by sharing information about the needs of the child at each age level and giving concrete examples of how mothers and fathers can provide excellent parenting as nurturers. The authors also made this book very easy to read by not going into great detail of research and professional language.

A theology of the cross is the core of this book on parenting. The promise of God in nurturing faith is "I will be with you always, even to the close of the ages." This is not a book that lists a number of ways one can become a perfect parent or that infers perfect parenting produces perfect children. A theology of the cross holds us accountable for our sin and acknowledges that being a family is messy business. Christian parenting is not about right ways, but about right relationships. Even when we fail and sin, our gracious God loves us, forgives us, and strengthens us to grow right next to each other and right next to God.

The Youth and Family Institute of Augsburg College has stressed in The Child In Our Hand conceptual model four imperatives for the ministry of the congregation and four keys for nurturing faith in the home.

Four Imperatives for Ministry of the Congregation

- Faith-focused education

- Strong, life-shaping families

- Congregation as family

- Christian youth subculture

Four Keys for Nurturing Faith in the Home

- Caring conversations

- Devotions in the home

- Family service projects

- Rituals and traditions

In this book the authors share ways parents nurture faith through the four keys listed above. Parents pass on stated values and faith through bonding with the child, the family atmosphere they create, the lifestyle they live, the rituals and traditions they develop and practice, and the boundaries that they create, express, and uphold.

The Youth and Family Institute of Augsburg College is pleased to bring you this first of **The Child In Our Hands Series.** We pray that it will be so helpful to families that they will look forward to the other parenting books to come in this series.

Dr. Dick Hardel, Executive Director

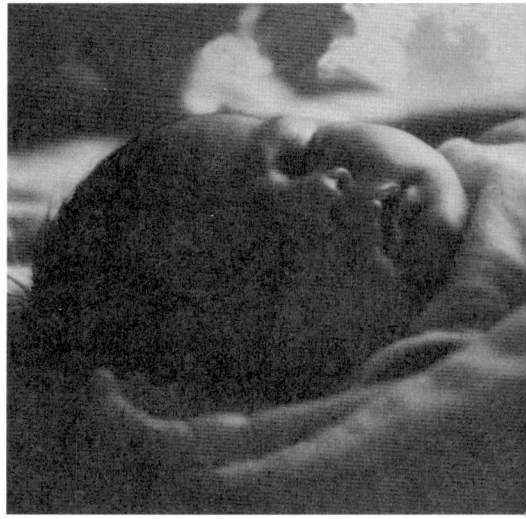

INTRODUCTION

A Contribution to Parental "Common Sense"

Most parents have their own ideas about raising children. These notions of child rearing are often grounded in a parent's experiences from childhood and expanded through their observations of other families and the media. Such learnings constitute parental common sense – a parent's most important resource in the care and guidance of children.

This book is written to support and supplement such parental common sense. It will put words to what parents already know as well as present them with new ideas. Reading this book will add to a parent's wisdom and offer alternatives to possible negative influences in a parent's views on bringing up a child.

This parental guide considers nurturing the faith and values of a child to be an essential task of parenting. Faith perspectives contribute to the vision for caregiving presented throughout. The faith and life issues most central to child-rearing are addressed. *Parenting With Purpose* integrates faith with the life of parents and children at every juncture of their relationship.

Each chapter concentrates on a specific aspect of a child's development and upbringing through the first six years. Part I provides a vision and core values for parenting. Part II focuses on parenting infants - birth through age one. Part III concerns rearing toddlers - ages two and three years. Part IV addresses the raising of young children - ages four through six years.

The material in the book will invite conversation among parents. Research shows that many parents – especially stay-at-home parents – often feel isolated and express a need to discuss their child's development and upbringing with others. Discussion groups composed of parents are supportive settings in which experiences and concerns can be shared as well as core commitments and good practice supported. Each chapter of *Parenting With Purpose* concludes with questions designed to generate such conversation.

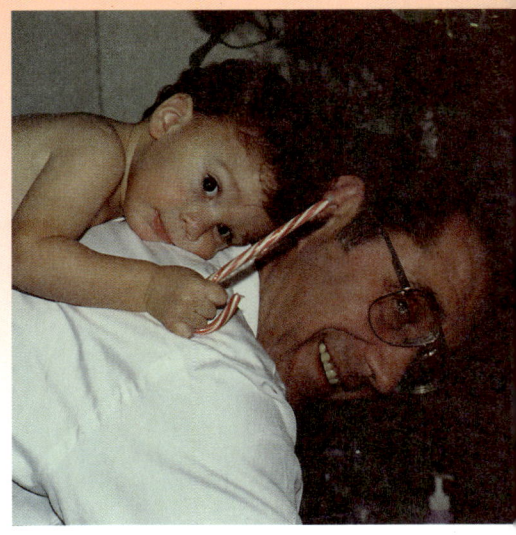

PART ONE:

Vision and CoreValues

CHAPTER ONE

Intentional Parenting and Caregiving

A child is literally placed in a parent's hands. Whether the new child arrives by birth or adoption, to have a child put into one's hands is to have fundamental responsibility for another person. An infant needs help to stay alive, for left to herself, the child will die. A child needs more than physical support and care however; she is also emotionally and socially, morally and spiritually dependent on the care and guidance of others in order to become independent and responsible.

BOTH PARENTS AND CAREGIVERS

Raising a child occurs in significant one-to-one interactions within an intricate web of caring people. Parents raise children. Communities of caregivers raise children. Families, peers and neighborhoods provide the many faces and variety of systems which shape a child's very being. Good child rearing requires the commitment and competence of both parents and community caregivers.

The responsibility involved with the arrival of an infant can be over-whelming to parents. As outside caregivers, it's important to offer help and support. As parents, it's important to accept support so that energies can be devoted to the newborn and each other. Help can come in many ways – errands run, care of a sibling or the new-born, meal preparation, and other household duties. When little Janie was born, neighbors Sean and Mai offered to take care of the baby for two hours so Tom and Kelly could spend some time alone with three-year-old Zoe. When two year old Sarah was adopted by Jessica, friends and neighbors brought dinners for two weeks...and stayed to talk with Jessica and play with Sarah.

A VISION OF A CHILD'S FUTURE

Parents and caregivers need a big picture within which to consider the many challenges and questions of child rearing. Such a frame-work and goals will enable parents to think more purposefully in specific situations. For example, if parents feel they should punish a child for something, it is wise to ask, "What will we accomplish by this punishment?" "Will this particular punishment serve the goals we have in bringing up our child?" "What will we teach the child through our actions?" "What attitudes will we convey?" The respons-es to such questions will best be determined by the vision and core values parents have for the child's upbringing.

PARENTS – PARTNERS WITH GOD

Christians have understood child rearing in the context of their rela-tionship with God. Understanding they are partners with God in raising a new human being, Christian parents and caregivers see child rearing as a high calling and responsibility.

In this Christian vision of child rearing, parents tend a child on behalf of God, for the mystery of life in the child flows from God who created and watches over the child.

Parents tend a child on behalf of the child. A child's emerging char-acter will be greatly influenced by the child's early life with parents and caregivers who have significant and life-long impact on those dimensions of the child's personhood that are not genetically coded.

Parents tend a child on behalf of the community. The community has a large stake in the child's potential whether as a constructive community contributor or a destructive social liability.

Parents tend a child for the sake of the kingdom of God. Jesus likened entrance to the kingdom of God to the trust evidenced in a small child. To tend children is to steward the Christian faith.

Because children carry the next generation's character, courage, and faith in their unfolding potential, parents tend a child for the sake of the future. Parents and caregivers provide primary roots and wings for their child's development — and through the child's development, humankind's future.

FAITHFULNESS

Parents and caregivers are to be guided in raising children by the faithfulness with which God relates to God's people. God cares. God makes and keeps promises. God persists. In Scripture God is there with and for humankind, Israel, Jesus Christ, and the Church. So it is to be among the generations, especially between parents and children. This faithfulness is dynamic; it is grounded in loyalty — in promised persistence. It is proactive; it respects and seeks the well-being of the other.

For men and women of faith, parenting is grounded in these core convictions that give confidence to parents, set direction for their efforts and establish their accountability before God, their children and the community.

Within this faithfully exercised, noble calling, parents will consciously or unconsciously operate from governing values that reflect a particular understanding of their children, their development and their care.

A CHILD

Some argue that a child is like a stone to be sculpted; others assert that a child is like a plant to be watered, pruned, and shaped; still others speak of a child as an animal to be trained. While all these metaphors contain helpful insights, none of them expresses the complexity of the growing child.

A child is a full, developing person in need of support and guidance. Out of the significant relationships with parents and caregivers this mysterious, impressionable, active life agent is forging his or her own and others' identity and character. To parent is to both evoke from and contribute toward a child's essential identity, ability, and character. In these interactions, the message the parent might well give the child is: "You are a person who is loveable, capable, and forgivable."

A child is loveable because God has created the child with inherent dignity: God loves the child, and the child belongs to God. Parents communicate this dignity and love to a child when they recognize and celebrate the mystery of the child's spirit. Children whose parents treat them with respect, learn to respect themselves and others. The more parents and caregivers value a child's uniqueness and elicit the child's gifts, the greater value and self-confidence the child develops.

As a parent works with a child to set realistic expectations, encourages the child to live up to those expectations, praises the child for success, and holds the child accountable for his or her own failure, the parent assists in the conversion of a child's latent abilities into effective life skills. A child needs challenges and coaching in order to become confident of capabilities for unfolding knowledge and skill for living independently and interdependently.

Every child experiences limitations and failures, even failure to live up to self-expectations. When grace is regularly experienced as acceptance and forgiveness, a child's dignity and abilities are secured and strengthened. A child who doesn't experience such grace becomes perfectionistic, fragile, or belligerent.

LIVING TOGETHER WITH OTHERS

Children have the potential to become both independent and interdependent. In order to do so, children need help both in standing alone and learning to live with others. Parents and caregivers can best assist children on their way to independence and interdependence by getting neither too far ahead nor too far behind children in their development. To bring up a child is not primarily doing something for or about the child, but to live life with the child.

Three-year-old Celeste may be disappointed that her new brother can't play with her. The parents should acknowledge this disappointment and then celebrate with her when baby Nick smiles at her. Then clap together and tell her how happy Nick is to have her for a sister.

LIFE ALONGSIDE THE CHILD

Child rearing is working out one's life alongside the child. Parents are responsible for tending their own lives with the maturity and competence that enhances their own wellbeing and contributes toward a healthy environment for a child. Parental competency in negotiating life's challenges and relationships fosters the social, psychological, moral, and spiritual atmosphere in which a child's life best unfolds. Effective parenting emerges from basic commitments to oneself, the child, and others that inform the thousands of day-to-day life choices and actions of the parents' and the child's common world.

Parenting and caregiving are at their core, conversing, working, and playing with children. It is important as early as possible to converse with children about their day, even, if at first children can only listen. When they are able, children can be expected to help care for themselves and join in performing household chores. In these activities children not only learn that all family members participate in common tasks, but also celebrate and support life with each other. In working and playing with their children, parents not only influence their offspring, but children change their parents. Bringing up children is primarily being a person with whom children can form a relationship in which children become confident, feel secure, and receive care.

NEGOTIATING RESPONSIBILITY

Child rearing is a unique way of living together, particularly in regard to responsibility. Even though, children and adults have equal human worth, they do not have the same responsibilities. In the beginning, parents and caregivers have complete responsibility for their children. As they grow, responsibility both for relationships with parents and others must be shifted to the children. Good parenting provides children solid relationships, good information, varied experiences, and honest engagement with life through which children can develop self-confidence, positive attitudes, faith, character, good habits, and values.

PARENTAL CHOICES AND VALUES

Even if parents are not conscious of passing values on to their children, they do so simply through the way in which they live with their children. Parental speech, attitudes, choices and behavior tell their children about the relative importance of work, play, possessions, relationships, etc. From the moment of conception and most especially from birth onward, parents are making choices that profoundly influence their children. It is impossible to be neutral with a child.

Leo Tolstoy's story "The Old Grandfather and the Grandson" provides a dramatic illustration of this parent-child life-1ab:

The grandfather had become very old. His legs wouldn't go, his eyes didn't see, his ears didn't hear, he had no teeth. And when he ate, the food dripped from his mouth.

The son and daughter-in-law stopped setting a place for him at the table and gave him supper in back of the stove. Once they brought dinner down to him in a cup. The old man wanted to move the cup and dropped it and broke it, The daughter-in-law began to grumble at the old man for spoiling everything in the house and breaking cups and said she would now give him dinner in a dishpan. The old man only sighed and said nothing.

Once the husband and wife were staying at home and watching their small son playing on the floor with some wooden planks; he was building something. The father asked: "What are you doing, Misha?" And

Misha said: "Dear father I am making a dishpan so that when you and dear mother are old, you may be fed from this dishpan."

The husband and wife looked at one another and began to weep. They became ashamed of so offending the old man that from then on they seated him at the table and waited on him.

Even though it is not easy to know what is best for a child, parents cannot wait for a child to become mature to make key decisions regarding the child's development and future. To avoid making decisions regarding a child's faith, character, attitudes and habits is to teach a child that these key elements of personhood are of little value to the parent and likewise to the child.

This is especially true regarding a child's faith and religious beliefs. Often parents, unsure of their own faith or believing that religion is an individual or private matter, avoid speaking about God or refrain from practicing their own faith with their child. In this choice and inaction parents are teaching their child that God is not important and engaged in the family's everyday life; for if faith were important, God would enter conversation, and children would be introduced to their parents' prayers, hymns, and worship.

This is also true for music, athletics, and literature. In these and other areas of life, children will one day choose for themselves what they value. But children cannot love music if they have never experienced fine music. They cannot enjoy a good book or exercise if they have never read or participated in athletics. Children cannot choose that of which they know nothing.

A CHILD'S CHOICES

While children lack the experience and maturity necessary to make major decisions for themselves, children thrive on choosing among options commensurate with their maturity. To give children well framed, regular choices teaches decision-making and deepens their investment in their relationships and their family's common life. For example, three-year-old Sammy and two-year-old Sara delight in choosing books to be read to them each evening before bedtime.

PREPARING FOR INDEPENDENCE AND INTERDEPENDENCE

If children are to be independent - to make their own choices- they must have a foundation on which to base those choices, as well as experience exercising their developing values and skills. If children are to be interdependent - to live effectively with others - they must have models as well as experiences in which to develop their knowledge and skills.

The child is placed in our hands. Our journey is a big part of their journey. Our responsibility is to give them the best we have of values and attitudes, knowledge, and skills so that they are equipped to walk life's journey on their own and with others.

CHILDREN LEARN WHAT THEY LIVE

An anonymous popular poem, regularly hanging on the walls in children's rooms captures this vision of child rearing:

If children live with criticism, they learn to condemn

If they live with hostility, they learn to fight

If they live with ridicule, they learn to be shy

If they live with shame, they learn to feel guilty

If they live with tolerance, they learn to be patient

If they live with encouragement, they learn to be confident

If they live with praise, they learn to appreciate

If they live with fairness, they learn a sense of justice

If they live with security, they learn to have faith

If they live with approval, they learn to like themselves

If they live with acceptance and friendship, they learn to find love in the world.

Although the cause and effect of each of the above situations may not always be true, the poem conveys how important a parent's actions are to the development of the child.

One might summarize this chapter with the following points:

TO BE PARENT OR A CAREGIVER IS TO:

• have responsibility for a full, yet developing human being;

• be the most important person in a child's life;

• celebrate a noble, God-given calling;

• give the child love and security;

• give the child encouragement and praise;

• see the child as lovable, capable, and forgivable;

• be an honest, mature, and genuine adult;

• share one's faith and values as one works out life with the child;

• be a model for the child; and

• prepare a child to make good choices and develop good relationships.

QUESTIONS FOR THOUGHT, CONVERSATION AND DISCUSSION:

1. Parents and caregivers have different opinions on raising a child.

   Parent A says: "I believe we must let children develop as freely as possible without trying to influence them. Parents should primarily provide for a child's basic needs and get out of the way."

   Parent B says: "I believe we must give children the knowledge and attitudes that give them direction in a diverse and confusing world. Parents should guide and influence a child toward what is best for the child."

   Do you agree or disagree with either of these parents?

   How would you express your understanding of the role of a parent?

2. Think about the sources from which you have received your ideas about raising a child. What do you consider to be the most important source and guide for your parenting?

3. To assume responsibility for a child deeply influences a parent's life. Share experiences of how your child has effected you and your relationships.

4. What are your core values regarding raising your child? Are there areas of parenting where you seek to be neutral? Are you succeeding? What message is this neutrality sending to your child?

CHAPTER TWO

Family Wellness

Families become units of life that have an existence uniquely their own. These life organisms become some of the most powerful influences in a child's life. One of the challenges of parenting is to know and shape these family crucibles.

Families take on their own particular form and within these structures carry out the functions that enable the family to survive. Within families concentrated forces interact to cause or influence change or development. Together, parents and children share a common world. This world becomes the crucible wherein children are brought up. One of the challenges of parenting is to know and shape this crucible. To do so is one of the most powerful parental roles in a child's life.

ELEMENTS OF FAMILY VITALITY AND RESILIENCY

As parents work to shape the family crucible, they can be guided by emerging information regarding strong families. There are key elements present in almost every family that are vital and resilient, no matter what its shape or circumstance. There are six traits of strong families.

1. Individuality

In strong families, all members are valued and free to be themselves. These families respect and encourage the uniqueness of each member. Parents don't have to agree on everything. Children don't have to all be the same or do the same things or excel at the same level or in the same way. Time is taken for the parent to be alone with each child, yet individuals also have time for themselves. Children are expected to think for themselves as they develop increasing capacities of independence and interdependence.

2. Solidarity

In strong families, parents and children are knowledgeable of, interested in, and loyal to each other. They invest in each other. They're open, share their experiences, and think and listen well. In these families, parents and children find and create times and ways to be together and connect with one another.

When parents spend important times with their children, they can strengthen the family's connections by sharing opinions, feelings, and beliefs; parents' transparency solidifies their humanness with their child and deepens the meaning and closeness of the entire family.

Parents can promote wellness in their families by regularly checking in with each other and their children throughout each day. When conflicts arise, they should take them up directly, giving consideration to all members of the family involved in the disagreement.

3. Adaptability

Strong families are open to new and different people and experiences. Parents and children, as well as the larger family constellation, are willing and able to respond to changes in composition, age, and situation.

Parents can enhance their family's and their children's comfort and competence with change by trying new things, encouraging their children to join them in the adventure, engaging fully in the journey, and celebrating or lamenting the results whatever they might be. Parents and children in strong families don't always see life in black and white. They develop new ways of coping. In these families parents allow their children to grow up. Roles change with age and life circumstances. Parents and children develop a clear and trusted process for solving problems together.

4. Continuity

In strong families, grandparents, parents, aunts, uncles, children, friends, etc. find ways of supporting one another when needed. They find ways of knowing and getting through tough times together. Parents can foster resiliency by responding in timely, accurate, and appropriate ways to the child's unique life struggles. For example, when the child gets a stomachache or doesn't want to go to nursery school, parents might be tempted to dismiss the child's signals by pampering or scolding the child. Instead, parents might enlist the child's feelings, thoughts, and courage in working through to an acceptable way of living with the struggle, defining the problem, finding a solution, etc. These situations in which a toddler struggles and parents respond, communicate the family's attitudes about facing and coping with difficulty.

Strong families develop habits, routines, celebrations, and traditions that draw them together and enable them to care for one another throughout the life cycle. Parents and children see themselves as a part of a historical, common life that shapes who they are.

5. Communication

Vital and strong families find their own ways to get through to each other no matter what the subject, no matter what it takes. When jokes are told or weird events occur, parents and children laugh together. When a parent or child is sad, they express concern, cry, spend time together, or hug and give each other time to heal.

Parents can encourage this effective exchange of meaningful life by their own honesty, openness, and humility with their children. Parents should make it clear that all subjects are valid for discussion and for tending by the family. This means it is important for parents to give attention to a toddler's curiosity and questions.

Young children are most satisfied and become strongest when they are allowed to face the full range of human experience from their level of perception and comprehension.

Families are communicating all the time, even in their silence and their absence from one another. Strong families encourage a wide range of communicating. Words are important. Gestures are given attention and are interpreted. Faces are valued windows of the soul. Silence and absence are noticed, allowed and taken up honestly and directly as honored elements in family exchanges.

Toddlers expand their worlds of both knowledge and exploration when their parents model and encourage honesty, variety, accuracy and respectfulness in their communication with others and the child.

6. A Life of Faith

Vital and resilient families share beliefs and values that constructively inform their day to day interactions, give direction to their lives, and sustain them in crises.

Parents who actively pursue their own spiritual quest and practice their faith, strengthen their own lives, the life of their family and that of their child. Public worship, personal study, individual prayer, serving others and connecting one's faith with one's daily life are all major contributions a parent makes to his family and child.

Toddlers are especially influenced by the spiritual attitudes and practices of parents and family. Hearing Mom or Dad pray about life, especially about her life, gives the child self worth, a sense of security and the confidence that she is loved. It also communicates to her that her family is included in the life and power of God who is bigger than her parents and her community.

FAMILY DYSFUNCTION

All families have their own mix of strengths and weaknesses. Some families are very flexible and communicate well, but have little continuity and stability. Some families have great solidarity, but little freedom for individuals to develop and grow.

In this mix of strengths and weaknesses, there are times and occasions when families become destructive for a particular person or persons, as well as to the entire family.

Sometimes these destructive dynamics come primarily from the ways the family interacts, such as when a parent physically or sexually abuses a child. Sometimes the dysfunction focuses primarily on the condition of one of the family members, such as when a parent is chemically dependent or depressed. Often the symptoms of the families' ill-health are not this dramatic or clear.

Whenever a parent experiences continuing mistrust, fear, despair, rage, sense of chaos, or manipulation, it is crucial for that parent to contact a trusted resource outside the family who can help them with the struggle. In most of these situations, the whole family will need attention, be relieved, and benefit greatly from competent assistance with its dysfunction. A competent family counselor will be a parent's best first-line of resources in these situations.

Research indicates that it is not what happens to a family, but what the family does with what happens to it, that determines the family's health.

DIVORCE AND FAMILY STRENGTH

Some marriages dissolve. Every divorce is painful and has significant impact on those involved. Honest and intentional work with the struggle of divorce helps family members heal and grow strong again. Without such tending of the issues around the divorce both the spouses and, if there are children, each of the children can sustain long-term ill effects from the break up of the marriage and the family.

Tending the grief and losses involved in divorce is important for both parents and children. Community and congregational resources are available to assist family members of all ages in these tasks.

Developing new ways of thinking, new ways of bonding, new primary relationships, and new family structures are crucial for parents and children living through a divorce. Knowledge and skills are available both from professional counselors and from families who have worked through these losses and moved on to a new and healthy life.

Working through the struggles of divorce and establishing a strong and healthy single parent family occurs best when family members tap trusted people available to share significant supporting roles in the emerging new family constellation. Congregations and family communities can be a rich pool from which to select these new trusted and adopted family members. Some congregations become single parent families' extended families of faith.

Working through the struggles of divorce very often results in parents, children, and their families developing vitality and resiliency they did not have before the marriage and family dissolved and reconstituted.

QUESTIONS FOR THOUGHT AND DISCUSSION

1. What were the strengths in your childhood family? Are those strengths still present in your extended family? How do these strengths influence your child?

2. Using the six traits of strong families cited in this chapter as clues, how might you as a parent add to the strength of your family? Who might support you in enhancing your family's strengths? Are there persons or learning opportunities in your community who could be of help?

3. In what ways is faith active in your family? Does it enhance the vitality and resiliency of your family in times of crises? In times of celebration? Are there faith traditions that are particularly effective in communicating the power and love of God in your family?

4. Are there destructive forces that are eroding your family's strengths and threatening its health? Who might help you deal with these destructive forces?

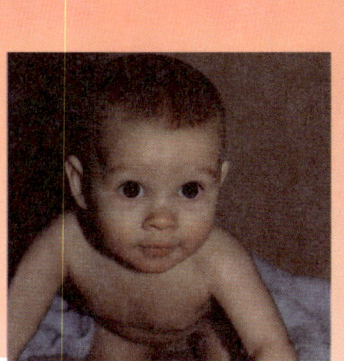

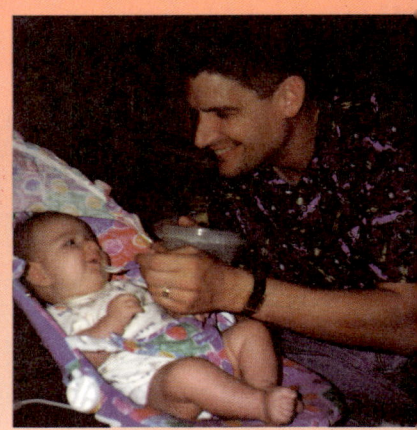

PART TWO:
Infants

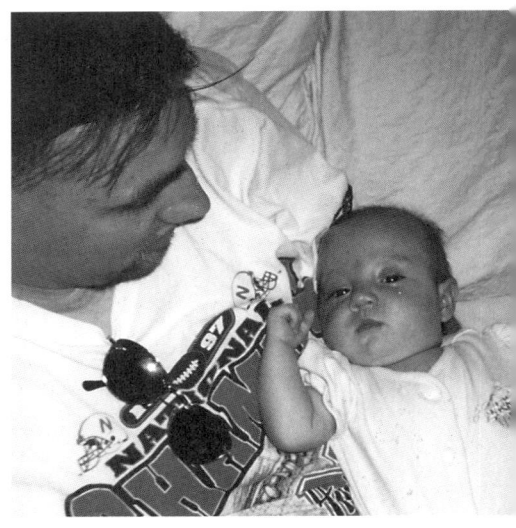

CHAPTER THREE:

The First Task: Attachment

Infants crave large amounts of time and attention. Yet, all the attention parents can give them is worth far more than the effort. Through caring and intimate contact, a foundation of knowledge and confidence is built for children, both in themselves and in their parents.

Birth is a huge adjustment! From the safe and warm comfort within the womb, a new person is suddenly thrust into an unknown world. Prior to birth, the mother's body takes care of all the child's needs. Suddenly, the tiny new body must breathe for itself, suck, swallow, digest, and excrete. Simultaneously, the child is besieged with strange, new stimuli of light and darkness, sounds and odors, people and objects.

PSYCHOLOGICAL PREGNANCY AND BIRTH

In the face of all that is new, the child must learn to adjust. It is not easy. She needed nine months of intimate physical connection with a mother before she came into the world. Now, whether she entered her family through birth, adoption, or foster care, she needs time for close contact with her parents and caregivers. Through this psychological pregnancy and birth a foundation is built for the child's relationship with herself and her surroundings.

During the first year of her life, the infant becomes acquainted with her parents and most significant caregivers and feels secure with them. She learns that her parents can be trusted, and that even if they leave her temporarily, they will return.

At the same time a child begins to learn about herself as an individual person. Even though it appears that an infant is unaware that she even exists, through growing awareness of and interaction with her surroundings, she becomes aware of herself as her own "I" person.

BASIC TRUST

Parents have an exciting task ahead of them as they become acquainted and attach with their child. While it is exhausting and parents may think the infant demands too much time and attention, this is a significant period of discovery for both the child and the parents. All caring, parental contact with the child strengthens the parent-child bond and is worth far more than the effort and hours expended.

Through caring interaction with the infant, a foundation is laid for the child's confidence both in herself and her parents. This basic bond and the resultant trust become the cornerstone of the structure on which the child's development and upbringing are built. Sally always talks and makes eye contact when changing Maggie's diaper. Maggie also communicates with Sally. They are building a strong bond of trust.

GREAT CHANGES

No other year in a person's life brings such great and rapid changes as a child's first year of life. For example, during this first year, the child's body length increases by 50%, and her body weight becomes almost three times her birth weight. This would compare to a ten year old adding between 25-30 inches to her height and 110-120 pounds of weight.

A new-born infant cannot even hold up her head. After a year, most children have already taken their first steps. From expressing themselves with screams, crying or gurgles, a one-year old child has begun to form distinguishable words.

These are changes that everyone can see and hear. But there are also great invisible changes such as a child discovering her surroundings and herself. It is important for parents to be attentive to the signals of these invisible changes, determine their meaning, and respond appropriately. Every day when John comes home from work, he looks forward to seeing what new things ten-month-old Annie has learned. When she repeats the new skill for her daddy, John responds with praise and hugs. Encouraged, she repeats it over and over.

INFANT AWARENESS

The newborn child often has been greatly underestimated. Infants understand more than has been previously thought.

Infants have been thought of as tiny, passive beings interested only in food, sleep, and comfort. Recent studies show that from his first breath, the infant is interested in the world around him. He is actually curious about what occurs within range of his senses. He actively searches for impressions and tries to arrive at a conclusion about his surroundings which soon take on meaning for him.

INFANTS NEED STIMULATION

The infant is occupied with anything that can stimulate her senses. She is especially interested in anything that can challenge and satisfy her need to master her surroundings.

This knowledge is significant for parents and caregivers as they enrich the immediate surroundings of the infant. A child must have opportunity to investigate for herself in order to satisfy her curiosity and need for stimulation.

Parents should remember this when they choose toys for their children. A child needs sounds, strong colors, and mobile objects that can develop her senses and thinking. Even as children have physical hunger, they possess a hunger of the senses and can become mal-nourished emotionally and psychologically without stimulation.

QUALITY INTERACTION WITH ADULTS

Infants have a basic need for contact with the people around them. One might call this contact wordless conversation. The child and adult speak with each other without words. Through glances, sounds, facial expressions, and touch, contact is made and communication occurs.

The importance of this type of conversation cannot be over estimated; through it the child and parents become acquainted. A close and emotional relationship is established which is fundamental for the child's further development and the parents' future attitude toward and impact on their child. Liz often stops what she is doing and gets down on the floor to talk to Avery about her surroundings. They are establishing the basis for future, comfortable communication.

MOTHERS, FATHERS, AND CAREGIVERS

Mothers are usually deeply engaged with their children. Mothers often breast-feed their children and take care of many of the child's basic needs. Previously, it was thought that an infant's attachment to his mother was due primarily to her bearing him, feeding him and satisfying his other basic physical needs. Recent studies indicate that nursing and feeding the infant are not in themselves the major factors in bonding with a child. More important for establishing caring and loving relationships with the child are emotional contact and stimulation. An infant loves the one who speaks to her, who caresses her, who sings to her and smiles at her. In short, it is the one who satisfies the child's emotional needs who bonds with the child and becomes a significant influence in the child's life.

Basic care and breast-feeding naturally provide much close contact and stimulation. A mother's milk is the best source of nourishment for an infant. But for mothers who cannot nurse their babies, for fathers, and other caregivers, it is important for all to know that they are capable of satisfying the child's important emotional and psychological needs.

The traditional role of mothers during infancy has created the myth that a father doesn't know how to care for a child. Fathers and other caregivers, as well as mothers, should participate in early interaction with the child. Fathers who initiate such contact will later be more engaged in their children's lives than those fathers who are not involved in the lives of their infants. While fathers cannot bear or breast-feed a child, these are the only things they cannot do for her. For both the sake of the child and her mother, a father should, if at all possible, participate in the child's first experiences of care. It is both a privilege and a responsibility for a father to participate in the daily feeding, clothing, caressing, and talking to his child.

QUALITY INTERACTION

The development of basic security for a child is not dependent on who cares for the child, but on how the child is cared for. That *how* is not primarily a question of pre-determined techniques, but rather a question of the commitments, attitudes, and quality of contact with the child on the part of the caregiver.

When a child cries, he sends a signal that demands a response. Is it food he wants? A diaper change? Physical contact? Sympathy? Comfort? Parents must learn how to be sensitive and discerning in responding to such signals from their child. It is an unfortunate misunderstanding that infants are spoiled if parents pick them up when they scream or cry. In the first three months of their lives, there is no question of spoiling a child. On the contrary, it is essential that the child receives immediate attention, contact, tenderness, and the warmth he craves, whether the signal is crying or smiling.

FAMILY EMOTIONAL CLIMATE

The quality of parental contact with a child is in part determined by the emotional climate in the family. Interaction with a child is part of the larger family communication and behavioral process. Therefore, relationships between the child's parents and significant caregivers are of vital importance. A warm and stable relationship between a child's father and mother, characterized by confidence and respect, is good not only for their marriage; this relationship is one of the most important sources of warmth and security the parents have to offer the child. If the child's parents are married, taking their marriage seriously is one of the most important contributions they can make to their child; if they are not married, it is important for them to develop a cooperative co-parenting partnership for the sake of their child.

Even at a very young age a child will be able to sense tension between her parents or other caregivers. Differences between two people are inevitable, but the way in which these differences are resolved will make a lasting impression on the child.

SHARING CAREGIVING RESPONSIBILITIES

For both married and single parents, close relationships with people in the larger family and community are important. It is necessary to look beyond one's own marriage and family for both giving and receiving support and care as well as friendship and security.

For a single parent, it is especially important to have help with baby sitting and friends or acquaintances who can be a surrogate father or mother. It is important for both single and dual parents to have other adults with whom to talk, especially concerning raising the child. If parents don't have built-in family and friends who provide this support, there are often community or church support groups that provide such help free of charge.

QUESTIONS FOR THOUGHT AND DISCUSSION

1. In 1900 a professional wrote the following in a magazine for women:

   Quiet, absolute quiet is necessary for the infant!

   Only feeding and bathing should disturb the child.

   If one knows there is no wrinkle in the clothes which is uncomfort-able to the child, or the child is not wet, one without a bad con-science can let the child scream. If its face is uncovered and its covers are light enough so that it can move freely, then a screaming session is nothing more than healthy motion.

   What view of infants is expressed in this quotation? What might a child care professional say about such a situation today? What do you think?

2. Parents find it natural from the first moment to talk to their infant, with or without words. What significance does such a con-versation have for the child? for the parent?

3. Some mothers boast about how well the father helps with the care of the their infant. Have you heard fathers who have boasted about how well a mother takes care of a child? How do fathers, mothers, and caregivers share child care in your family?

4. What are the unique challenges that arise for a single parent in caring for an infant? How can families and others be of help and support in a single parent family? How might single parents invite others into the care of their child?

CHAPTER FOUR
Security and Trust

An infant has a unique personality that is evident from birth. In the web of the child's development and first relationships both child and caregivers greatly influence one another, bringing dramatic change to each of their lives.

A CHILD'S UNIQUE CHARACTERISTICS AND CHANGES

Parents soon learn about their child and her pace of development. In the same interactions through which parents get to know their child, the child becomes acquainted with her mother or father. A rhythm of interaction develops in which both parent and child delight in communicating with one another. Parents notice new sounds, smiles, and activities. There is much in the child to give them joy.

From these early signs, parents expect to see their child develop according to a particular pattern and schedule. These first observations can make parents uneasy. They may wonder: "Is something wrong if my child is developing slowly?" There are differences in how quickly children grasp new information and master new skills.

A child can develop more slowly than the norm without there being any cause for concern. However, if the child fails to progress, it is important that the symptoms be looked at as soon as possible, for early detection provides the best opportunity for effective response to difficulties. During regular examinations by a physician these concerns should be raised and discussed.

Parent's are often amazed by the pace at which an infant grows and changes. This development does not happen automatically, however. A child needs a proper diet in order to grow physically healthy and strong. In like manner, the child's senses and mind also need nourishment and stimulation. This development occurs best when the child lives in a stimulating environment and has positive contact with people.

TOYS

Very soon, a child grasps for anything in her reach. However her motor skills must have time to develop and she needs practice in order to control her hands and fingers. Toys that a child can hold and manipulate are instrumental in this important physical growth. Toys also enhance a child's intellect and whet a child's curiosity. The more potential uses for the toy, the more creativity is cultivated in the child.

A child is gratified when a toy responds to her efforts. For example, if a rattle makes noise when the child shakes it, the child smiles with a sense of accomplishment. Consequently, the number of toys available to a child is not as important as the type of toys; it is more important that toys will challenge the child and give her a desire to look for new ways of utilizing them.

SECURITY IS LEARNED

To respond well to new challenges, the child must feel secure and self-confident. This is the key to a child's development. Through contact with trustworthy parents, the child not only experiences security, but comes to trust his father and mother and at the same time learns to trust himself and his ability to respond to challenges.

The foundation for this security and confidence in himself and others is established during the first year of life.

Smiles and jabbering are the first signs that a child is beginning to feel safe with the people around him. Another sign is his ability to follow others in the room with his eyes. This period of a child's development when he learns this security and trust is extremely critical. During this period a child needs large amounts of close contact with a limited number of adults.

PARENTS AS THE BASE OF SECURITY

Gradually, the child learns to connect herself to her closest family members. In the beginning, a child does not react negatively to strangers. But within a few months there is a difference. She becomes more tentative and skeptical. She may scream and cling to her mother or father when strangers are around. She might cry when a mother or father leaves.

This strong attachment to mother or father or closest caregivers is a good sign. Protesting separation from parents or close caregivers indicates a child is developing a base of security. Such a base is necessary for the child to risk exploring the world around her. When doing so, she will return to her parents to replenish her feelings of security.

How does a parent become a security base for a child? First, parents can look for signals from the child and respond when he smiles, cries, jabbers or in any other way communicates with them. Secondly, parents can create a warm and friendly climate in the child's home.

During this time, contact between the child's mother and father contribute much to the security of the child. If the child's parents are married, this means maintaining quality in their marriage as well as assisting each other in caring for the child. Helping each other with the many tasks necessary in caring for the child and the household are excellent means of establishing a friendly and caring atmosphere for the child and family. Brad and Deb take turns with certain, regular child care responsibilities, such as diaper changes, baths, walks, and bedtime prayers. The children have learned that they can depend on both Mom and Dad for love and care.

PARENTS MUST CARE FOR THEMSELVES

Even though parents have a child to care for, they still have their own lives to tend and in most cases their marriage and careers to maintain. The newborn child often takes so much time and energy that parents can easily forget about themselves and each other. Not only infants, but parents and their marriages also need care and attention.

Parents need regular times away from their infant child for the sake of the child, themselves and each other. When parents are rested and fresh, they are better caregivers. When mother and father are supportive of and delight in each other, they create a secure environment and have more to offer their child.

The need for time away from the child is equally as important for single parents. It is necessary to get away just to survive. All parents might see relatives, neighbors or friends as potential partners in raising their child. Relaxation away from home will create new energy and creativity in the parent, which, in turn, helps the child as well. These mini-vacations can greatly add to vitality and tenderness in the family. Kae's church offers free child care for three hours one evening a month so that parents who don't have help available can enjoy a night out with each other. Parents are asked to register in advance, as space is limited and so sufficient, reliable help will be available for the safety of the children.

A CHILD'S BAPTISMAL JOURNEY

A child is born into the human family; she is born into a particular family and joined genetically and relationally to her parents. Yet, she must become intimately acquainted with her parents in order to feel secure and experience trust.

Such is a child's relationship with God. Through baptism a child is born into God's family and adopted into the body of Christ to live in relationship with God and God's people. Yet, the child must become acquainted with Jesus Christ and God's people in order to experience security in Jesus and have confidence in God.

AN INFANT'S FAITH

What is faith in the life of an infant … in one who is not aware of his baptism and who will not, for a long time understand stories or even songs about God?

A child becomes acquainted with mother and father through contact and play. This occurs long before he can understand words and concepts. In the same way, he will also learn about God. Through a secure relationship with mother and father, the child will learn about a God who cares and is faithful.

This confidence that is created during the first year of life provides an important foundation for a child's confidence and trust in God. An infant's contact and conversation with God occur through other people. As parents read or sing evening prayers beside the crib, they pray both for and with their child. Thus the child is introduced to God and provided an opportunity to gradually discover what it means to pray.

Parents need not be religious experts to read basic Bible stories, to sing simple children's songs with a tape, and to speak honestly of their life to God in prayer. Through this basic practice of faith, both parents and children become better acquainted with God.

Each evening Emily and Nathan say their "God blesses" with one of their parents. They simply go down the list of people who are important to them, saying "God bless Joyce," "God bless Joel," "God bless Liz," "God bless Amy." Prayer has become a very comfortable and personal thing.

QUESTIONS FOR THOUGHT AND DISCUSSION

1. The following dimensions are examples from the famous Chess and Birch study. In this research project, 250 children were care-

fully observed from birth through childhood. From the very beginning, characteristic differences were found among the children in many areas for instance:

a. Activity level - from completely calm to very active.

b. Sensitivity - from those who were very aware of sounds and light, to those who appeared to be oblivious to these stimuli.

c. Intensity of Response - from those who expressed themselves loudly and strongly to those who cried softly or smiled faintly.

d. Adaptability - from those who easily adjusted to any change to those who had a difficult time with any change.

e. Rhythmicity - from those who appeared to be born with an inherent schedule to those whose responses were chaotic and unreliable.

Which characteristics describe your child in regard to these abilities?

2. This chapter discusses the importance of young infants acquiring basic trust in themselves and their surroundings. This trust is dependent on the child's awareness of security realized primarily through their parents. How can you as a parent be a base of security for your child?

3. A child can acquire basic trust through his parents. A child can also learn confidence and trust in God. What can parents do so that the child will learn this basic trust?

4. Name three or four typical toys for infants and evaluate the contribution they might make to a child's development.

CHAPTER FIVE

Closeness, Distance, and Absence

Attachment to an adult encourages love in a child. He learns to love those who care for and are close to him with a deep, bonded love.

ATTACHMENT

Closeness and attachment are two necessary elements of an infant's early life and development. An infant needs close and secure contact with her family. This contact consists not only of regular physical presence, but also of interaction with her parents through touching and holding, eye contact, conversation, and concentrated attention. Through this closeness, the parents become a base of security as the child grows and unfolds.

These close connections generate love in the child. She learns to love her closest family with a deep, bonded love. She will want her caregivers for herself alone. She will want to be in their presence, touch them, pull their noses, stick her hand in their mouths. It is almost as if the child wants to own them. Although the child's tremendous need to be with them can be tiring, these love declarations are to be welcomed!

SEPARATION MUST BE LEARNED

At this point a child can act like a little dictator not wanting to let his parents out of his sight. When a parent leaves him, he may pout or scream. It's as if he cannot accept the fact that his parents will not be with him every minute. Yet he must learn to separate from his parents in order to be independent.

To become independent is a long and difficult process - a process that lasts throughout childhood and into the teenage and young adult years. As soon as the child begins to cling to his parents, he must begin to learn acceptance of their occasional absence.

This can be a painful lesson to learn. Gradually, the child must learn that "If Mom leaves me, she will soon be back again." A child learns to live with this separation primarily through experience. When time after time the child experiences that Mom and Dad really do return to him, he becomes more and more convinced that he can trust them.

The child's experiences with his parents' comings and goings creates an inner certainty that his parents exist, even if they are not in his presence continuously. By being closely tied to his parents and steadily experiencing that they return again and again, he is also gradually building basic trust in himself and the world around him. This confidence is the basis for healthy psychological and moral development.

UNUSUAL SEPARATION STRESS

Sometimes separation from her parents can put an unusual strain on a young child. Parents should, first of all, remember that all children develop at different rates, and that includes how they handle separation. However, if parents feel their child is experiencing an unusual amount of separation stress, they might ask themselves two questions: "With whom are we leaving our child?" and "How often are we leaving our child?"

If the child is left with people who are strangers, she may react with screams and protests, and later become passive and depressed. If a child stops screaming or protesting, it does not necessarily mean that her fear is gone. On the contrary, silence and passivity can be signs of uncertainty and anxiety. It is best if parents leave their child with someone the child has had an opportunity to get to know and trust in her parents' company. Taking along a familiar or favorite toy or blanket can be helpful and comforting to the child as well.

If a child experiences separation too often, she develops lack of confidence in herself and the world around her. How often is too often? Again, this will vary from child to child. The important thing to remember is that parents should spend good, quality time with their child to encourage the self-confidence needed for separation. When she has developed a strong bond with one or more people who give her care, she can bear more separations. The safer she feels, the more separations she will be able to endure.

DIFFICULTIES WITH SLEEP

Many small children have difficulties going to sleep and sleeping. Sleepless nights with a screaming infant can be a nightmare for parents. During the first months of a child's life, sleepless nights can be the result of hunger, colic, and other physical discomforts. Sleep also means separation from parents. Therefore, the more secure and confident a child, the more able he will be to handle the separation from his parent that comes at bedtime and during the night.

Infants must learn the rhythms of day and night, especially the quietness of the night. In order to learn this, a child must be both physically and relationally comfortable. After a long and tiring work day, finding quality time for the child at bedtime can be difficult. Because bedtime is so important, as far as possible, parents should develop bathing and bedtime preparation rituals that satisfy a child's needs for togetherness, play, and physical closeness.

When a child wakes and screams in the night, he is often calmed simply by knowing that a parent is there. However, for both the child's and their own good, parents must set limits. If there is nothing wrong, as a general rule a child is able to scream longer than parents can bear to listen! A good rule of thumb is to check the clock regularly. What a parent thought to be a half an hour was perhaps but ten minutes — all children need to learn to adapt to the rhythms of parents' presence and absence, of parents' rhythms of day and night.

If encouraged, most children will get on a schedule within three months after birth. If bedtime and sleep disruptions persist, parents should consult their pediatrician for professional counsel.

DAILY RHYTHMS OF PRESENCE AND ABSENCE

While placing a child in a day care center or leaving her with a babysitter for the first year of her life is not ideal, it may be necessary for some parents. When the child must be separated from parents a whole day, it is important that her relationship with the babysitter or personnel in the care center is as stable and permanent as possible. Intentional, cooperative efforts which deepen and coordinate the care given by both the caregiver and the parents are important in developing stability in these relationships and the child's sense of security.

Parents with a child in day care might well establish close contact every day with their child by taking ten to fifteen minutes upon arriving home and again at bedtime to focus fully on their child and give her their undivided attention. By setting aside these rituals of engagement upon rejoining one another and saying "good night" before sleep, a parent frames the evening with the quality interaction that becomes a highlight of the day and deepens the parent's attachment to the child.

If, in her first twelve months, the child acquires the necessary foundations of confidence and security, she will later be well equipped to handle daily absences from her parents.

OTHER ADULTS

A child can learn to relate well with people outside his family. During the period when he is bonding with his parents, he will naturally be more skeptical and anxious around strangers. Even a grandparent can be considered a stranger. But the more secure he becomes with his family and primary caregivers, the more he will be able to negotiate relationships with other people.

EXPLORATION

Confidence and security give a child courage to use her emerging knowledge and skills. She will enjoy using newly acquired control over her hands, fingers, feet, and body that she strives to master.

Everything within reach in the house is of interest and invites investigation. A child eagerly grabs things, picks them up, throws them down, opens drawers, pulls off table cloths, even eats the dog's food. A child wants to explore everything within her reach. And as she learns to crawl, stand and walk alone, her boundaries widen.

Not all children are equally active. They vary greatly in the ages at which they initiate and master activities. Whether a child reaches out for a rattle at 6 weeks or 12 weeks or walks at 9 months or 19 months, she needs security, opportunity, and encouragement to do the things she can manage.

BOUNDARIES

It is for the safety of a child, as well as for the sake of valued objects on household shelves, that it is necessary to establish boundaries. From the beginning, a "No, No!" should leave a definite impression. When the child approaches an electrical outlet, a parent's "No, No!" should be connected to removal to a safer place. Limits are best learned through these concrete experiences.

Sometimes a "No" means that a child will be disappointed and feels he has lost something. Such experiences are not harmful and are important discoveries for a child. It is important that the child be taught the reason behind the "No, No!" If he learns the reason behind the rule, he will feel more secure, respected and loved.

"No - No's" should be accompanied by alternatives. A child needs constant exposure to something new to be explored, preferably something that will challenge his senses, mind, and body. Everything that is indestructible by small hands and safe can be available for investigation.

Hardly anything amuses a toddler as much as pots, pans, and their lids. Many small children have a preference for such cooking utensils over their expensive toys. Toys that make sounds, however, are always popular. As the child develops, toys that invite participation and utilization best encourage a child's imagination and motor skills. In these moments a child begins the discovery of meaning in life, long before he knows the words and wonders, "Why am I alive?"

This poem written by Else-Lill Berglund expresses a child's pre-language experience of key values and meaning:

WELCOME TO THIS WORLD

You are welcome to this world
You have the right to a name,
an identity and membership in
the human family.
You are welcome into our family.
You are unique and special.
No one has ever been like you.
No one will ever be like you.
You are allowed to be who you are.
You do not need to be perfect
to be loved by us.
You have the gift of life, and all
life is holy and valuable.
This is part of your life.
You have the right to have needs.
And to announce your needs.
You have a right to care, happiness
and growth.

GOD IS CLOSE BY

A child becomes acquainted with and attached to her parents through close contact. Through such concrete experience with powerful, caring adults, a child also learns about God and God's presence. Bedtime with its activities is an important time to celebrate this parent-child, God-child, closeness. Holding a child and reading a simple story or singing a song fosters warmth and care. Praying evening prayers names God's presence and enhances the child's security. Bedtimes, meal times, laptimes and sick days are moments when a young child and her parent can experience such closeness to one another and God.

QUESTIONS FOR THOUGHT AND DISCUSSION

1. What type of child care or babysitting does your child have? How have you come to decide on this arrangement? If long separations are necessary, what are you doing to foster stability and encourage attachment to the child's key caregivers? What positive results come to both parents and child when a child spends time with a caring, competent and consistent babysitter?

2. How might one rearrange one's home so that the "No, No! things" can be exchanged for "Yes-things?"

3. Infant Sarah has been unable to sleep at night. Time after time she is picked up, but she screams again every time she is returned to her bed. Mom and Dad are tired and frustrated. What might be going on? Have you had experiences such as this? What would you do in this situation?

4. The bedtime routine is a time for quality parent-child contact and closeness. Can you remember good-night rituals from your own childhood? Did you have favorite activities? Do you have music you might play for your child to settle and calm him? What Bible story and other storybooks are appropriate for your child at his or her age?

PART THREE:
Toddlers

CHAPTER SIX

Discovering the World

For a one-year old child, the world is unexplored territory. Gradually, as the child's experience expands, her horizon widens. New areas have to be explored and more territory conquered. A one-year old child is everywhere at once and into everything.

Around twelve months, an infant becomes a toddler. Huge, fast-paced changes have occurred during the first year of the child's life. The child is now physically three times larger than at birth. As an infant she lay in her parent's arms, dependent on them and other caregivers for every need; her most basic life tasks were surviving and growing closer to her parents. Now this little person is moving away from her parents into a life of her own. Her body is full of buoyancy and her mind with the adventure of life.

FROM DEPENDENCE TO INDEPENDENCE

The child's objective now is to become more independent. He becomes more aware that he exists, that he is uniquely himself, independent of his parents.

It is remarkable that the path to independence passes through dependence. As an infant, a child learns dependence on his parents in order to become confident and expand his awareness of the world. As before, in this new journey toward independence, communication with his parents is still important. Mom and Dad are the sources to whom he must return to replenish his own inner security and confidence. While drawing on his reservoir of trust, he now requires other stimuli and challenges to utilize his own resources and develop his own possibilities.

The child's struggle toward independence vacillates from day to day. One moment it's as if he says, "I can manage it myself;" and in the next moment, he cries for security and comfort with his parents. A parent's role is to seek balance between these contradictory feelings and impulses within the developing child. Even as a child will drop his parent's hand and try something alone, the opportunity to return to the safety of the parent's hand must be available.

EXPLORATION

While a toddler needs stimulation and challenges, she is not passive. She is actively influencing her surroundings, both by what she does and how she does it. Through her actions, she learns about herself and the world around her. This happens first and foremost as she explores and discovers new people, abilities, and objects.

ON A JOURNEY OF DISCOVERY

For a one-year child, the world is unexplored territory. Gradually, as the child's experience expands, his horizon widens. New areas have to be explored and more territory conquered. It is not unusual for a one-year old child to be everywhere and into everything at once.

While a toddler is not always easy to follow, a parent must be close at hand to set limits and give the child security. As far as the child is concerned, there are no limits. If no one stops him, he will head for the stairs or the street. He has no inherent understanding of danger or safety, right or wrong; there is no inborn brake system.

Here as elsewhere in child rearing, balance is important. The child must be allowed to unfold naturally; on the other hand, he must learn of dangers and that which is not allowed. "No, no!" "Stop right there!" "Don't touch that!" "Don't go up there!" are constant repetitious sounds in the little explorer's ears. Even if a parent says, "No," ten times when the child pushes the television remote buttons, the child has forgotten the following day because the knobs fascinate him. Parents sometimes feel like giving up. Won't the child ever learn? Yes, of course he will; but it takes time. It is not easy when the child does not yet understand words and cannot remember long. Repeated, concrete experiences are required before what is dangerous and unsuitable takes hold in the child's memory.

Toddlers can not think into the future. Therefore it is difficult for him to wait even one second for something. When he wants something, he wants it now. He may cry when he gets jam on his fingers, but still protests when a parent tries to wash him. Toddlers are people-of-the-moment. This is a great advantage for parents because it is also easier to distract the child from something dangerous and get him interested in something else.

WORDS ARE DISCOVERED

When a child discovers that people and things have names, she has a major instrument for thinking. At the same time, parents possess a new tool for communication with their child. Sounds have been familiar to the child from the beginning. She has jabbered and created her own sounds and her caregivers have jabbered in return. Parent and child have, in a manner of speaking, understood each other. What is new is that the child has discovered that the word "mama" means her mama. The child points to the lamp and says "amp" or she pats the dog and says "ow-wow." She has discovered one can substitute words for things, especially when one speaks and thinks.

In the beginning, words cover a multitude of things. "Ow-wow" can mean dog, cat, or other animals. More experience is necessary before a child understands that every four-legged animal is not a dog.

If a child is to discover the intent of the sounds, she must have the chance to discover both the words and what the words stand for. To understand what the word dog actually means, she will have to be aware of dogs, not only one, but several.

The best foundation for her new skill must be constructed of varied experiences. A child learns to understand both the specific and the abstract — what it is to be kind, good, helpful, considerate, to forgive others, and so on — only through many experiences and much practice.

Children experience words long before they understand what the words stand for. But perhaps they understand more than we are aware of. Books are an excellent aid in understanding those words and learning to use them in conversation. Story-reading time with a child on one's lap is of great value and cannot be emphasized enough. While sitting safely within the warm and tender arms of a loving parent, a child both strengthens the attachment with her parents and makes great strides in understanding words through pictures and sound.

GOD'S STORIES AND SONGS

It is important that learned words are applied to a child's experiences of God. If the word God is to be something besides meaningless sound, the child must experience God in conversations, stories and songs with his parents. When a parent prays with a child he will think of God as a person. He will discover that God is close by and that he, as well as his parents, can talk to God, even if God can't be seen.

It appears that children can experience God long before they understand words in prayer. They experience with and from their parents' calmness and reverence something that is different than their other experiences.

If this is to happen, the life of faith within the family should be both articulated and practiced, becoming something the child can discover. For example, when parents pray in the presence of the child at bedtime, they give him the chance to meet and discover God in the rhythms of daily life.

Parents can sing or say prayers and grace at mealtime. It is a good idea to use a variety of prayers and prayer topics, praying in one's own words as well as using classic children's prayers or Psalms. The critical elements, however, are reverence and genuine encounter with God, which the child hears and learns to respect. Some parents may think it is difficult to pray, perhaps because they feel their faith is unreflected or rarely articulated, but parents should remember that God is gracious and great enough to hear our prayers, no matter where we are in our faith. Plus, as a child experiences his parents' conversation with God in good times and bad, in both church and home, he learns more of God's presence and action in all of life.

QUESTIONS FOR THOUGHT AND DISCUSSION

1. What does it mean to say the road to independence goes through dependence?

2. Toddlers learn through exploring the world. How does a child learn during these explorations? Give examples of how parents can encourage and support a child's learning through exploration.

3. How can parents assist their child with the basics of language?

4. When parents pray evening prayers, a child has opportunity to experience faith in practice. How do you see yourself doing this with your child? What is most natural or comfortable or possible for you?

CHAPTER SEVEN

Self-Awareness and Personal Identity

The toddler is in an important discovery phase.

It is exciting to see how he investigates things around him and learns to fit words to them. At the same time, he is at the point of making the most important discovery of his life: "I am Me!" He begins to learn that he is an "I" person -- a person who knows that he both can and will perform definite actions. This is the basis for teaching him to take initiative and responsibility in becoming an independent and interdependent person.

A child's months as a toddler are important in developing independence. A child will begin to create a picture of herself during this "me" phase. This self-image is immensely important for her development. A parent's important role during these months is to support this new found independence, while at the same time helping the child to realize and accept her interdependence with those around her.

THE DEVELOPING SELF

Development of the self begins as the child discovers his own body - that the hand is "my hand," the foot is "my foot," "my head," etc. This development of the self can easily be followed by watching the child recognize himself in the mirror. Early in his first year, the mirror is fun for him because it reflects his own movements. Bit by bit he begins to understand that what he sees in the mirror does not come from within the mirror itself. He gradually understands that the mirror reflects a picture of himself. A parent can test this development by putting a mark on the child's nose and letting him look at himself in the mirror. If the child points to the mark on his nose, he has begun to know his face and what he looks like. More time may be needed, however before he understands who it is he sees in the mirror.

Words, especially the child's name come into play at this juncture in self-development. It is helpful for a child to hear, "Where is Bobby's nose?" "Where are Bobby's eyes?" In this "game," Bobby begins to experience his own body as part of himself. Soon the child will use his own name when he speaks about himself.

THE EMERGING WILL

The words "I", "me", and "mine", once taken into use by the child, are heard more and more often! These words are used constantly with "will" or "will not." This is a certain sign that your child is discovering his own will. This discovery is a milestone in self-development.

Willfulness becomes most noticeable when the child opposes requests from parents. At this stage, parents often think their child looks on every suggestion or directive from them as a threat against her own will! So the child decides that even if she means "yes," it is better to say "no" so as to protect her emerging self.

The words "me" and "mine" are used routinely during the day's regular activities such as eating, washing, brushing teeth, etc. The child grabs the wash cloth, spoon, or toothbrush to show herself and everyone else that she can and will do it herself.

THE CHILD AS PROTESTER

To their chagrin, first-time parents often find themselves now, on a collision course with this child who was once so helpless and amenable. He is now determined to show how independent he is by doing exactly the opposite of what his parents say. If parents regard this stage as rebellion and gather their forces to put down the insurrection, they create trouble both for themselves and the child. It is tiring, frustrating, and can sometimes leave parental nerves and patience in tatters. But this is not a power struggle where parental prestige is at stake unless parents make it one. It is more accurate and meaningful to regard the child's declaration of independence as a necessary step in his development of self awareness and independence.

It does not mean that the child should always be allowed to do what he wishes. Experiencing and setting limits are necessary components in her self-development. It is best if instructions and limits are kept simple and consequences are clear. For example, eighteen-month-old Derek is told he must not throw the modeling clay at his sister. If he does, he will not be allowed to play with the clay for the rest of the day. When he throws the clay, Mom calmly removes him from the play area, restating the rule and its consequence. Another day when he plays nicely, Mom praises him for his good behavior.

PARENTS AND CAREGIVERS AS MIRRORS

Parents play an important role in the development of the picture the child has of herself. Parents function as a mirror for a child. A parent's words and ways of responding are signals to the child as to how she is to act and be. A child who regularly meets criticism and other negative reactions, learns early in life to think "I can't...," "I'm bad," "I'm dumb." A negative self image like this will easily take root and be reinforced through repeated and self-fulfilling experiences. A vicious circle develops: "I cannot," with it's companion "I won't try." In this cycle the child's negative self-image is confirmed and becomes more difficult to change.

The cycle of reinforcing child's self image can also be positive. It occurs when parents send positive signals each time an opportunity arises. When a child tries to use a spoon, it seems more natural for parents to be concerned about the mess the child makes than about the fact that she actually manages to put part of it into her mouth! Self-confidence is created, however, through experience in mastering an act. Parental affirmation along the way to mastering a skill can serve to further confirm the growing positive self image.

UNEQUAL POWER – EQUAL WORTH

Children's feelings of equal worth should not be based on what they are able to perform. Their capacities vary greatly in developing and mastering various activities. This is especially evident in physical and language skills. One is easily tempted to compare a child with siblings, cousins, and other children. Children must be assured that parents love them and that they are valuable regardless of what they are able to do.

CHILD OF GOD

The Bible teaches that all people are created by God. This helps parents see that a child has limitless worth and that all are equally worthy or unworthy. Therefore all children have the right to be loved and appreciated. In relation to God, persons are valued - even when they are unable to live up to expectations. Whether children or adults, all people need forgiveness and the possibility to start anew.

I AM
- created by God and have unlimited worth;
- unique with a great many possibilities;
- what my parents mirror that I am;
- so valuable that parents look at me, listen to me, and touch me;
- what I have opportunity to choose;
- what I dare to do;
- a person who can do things for herself;

- one who receives encouragement and praise
  for what I do;
- as self-confident as my parents dare to be;
- baptized and a child of God.

QUESTIONS FOR THOUGHT AND DISCUSSION

1. In a 1920's book on parenting, it is written: "The child whose willfulness is met and bent by strong parental will as early as infancy will have an advantage that will serve him all his life."

   What is your understanding of a child's willfulness? How might parents respond constructively to a child's willfulness?

2. This chapter asserted that a child's self-development is literally reflected in a child's response to seeing himself or herself in the mirror. Have you played the mirror game with your child? How did he or she respond? In what ways is the child's self image dependent on caregivers as mirrors.

3. It has been said: "I will become what I think I am." What does this say about the significance of a small child's self-image in further personality development?

4. Re-read the points under the title: "I am." Which of these coincide with your own self-image? Which will you especially try to promote in your own children's self-development?

CHAPTER EIGHT

The Child and God

Is it possible to include God in our relationships and conversations with young children?

GOD - PARENTAL UNDERSTANDINGS

Through baptism, God has done something important in the child's life. God has received her and made her God's child. This happened although the child understood nothing of the ceremony.

A child is born into the world without understanding how it happened. Parents care for their child long before the child understands either the care or who her parents are. Parents are parents regardless of how the child feels or thinks of them. That's the way it is with God. God is just as real, regardless of whether a child does or does not understand.

However, how and what a child comes to think of God is important for the shape and depth of her relationship with God. Therefore, a child must become acquainted with God -- as God really is.

A child learns about God first through her parents. Her thoughts about God and images of God are dependent on parents' relationship to their child and to God.

UNCONDITIONAL LOVE

The parent-child relationship is one of the most prevalent biblical illustrations of the relationship between God and humans. The Bible describes God both as a father who cares for his children and a mother hen who protects her chicks under her wings. God loves all children even when they don't return that love. God wants what is best for all people and loves all people regardless of how or what they are. God's love is unconditional.

Even though parents will not always love unconditionally, these illustrations in the Bible give parents models for the preferred parent-child relationship. Parental love for their children can be strengthened and inspired by God's love for both parents and children. If children are to develop in a healthy and positive way, they must feel safe in their parents' love for them.

In this positive experience of parental love a foundation is laid on which can be built the image of God as a good and loving parent. Whether they know it or not, for good or ill, parents become a model for their children's emerging image of God.

GIVING AND RECEIVING LOVE

Usually no one loves a child as much as his parents. Yet, it is not always easy for parents to carry out this deep love in a positive way.

For a toddler of eighteen months it is important that parents demonstrate their love through care and closeness. In concrete and physical ways a child needs to know that parents love him through touching and bodily contact. There is no reason to limit the hugs parents give their child when he seems to be particularly vulnerable and needs them. Taking a child into one's lap and talking, reading, or singing to him are equally important bodily contacts. Bathing a child can also become physical contact that is an expression of parental love.

Physical contact is important in giving a child concentrated attention. Appropriate bodily contact makes it easier to concentrate one hundred percent on the child, and concentrated attention tells a child that he is loved.

EYE CONTACT

Eye contact is another way to give concentrated attention to a child. Eyes are one of a parent's most important tools for contact and closeness. Children's eyes are like radar antennae searching for another pair of eyes. Will they make contact? What kind of answer will they receive? Often parents use eye contact unconsciously in order to transmit feelings to children. Parents often and easily look into their child's eyes to send negative messages. It is even more important to use eye contact when the child needs encouragement and praise. The emotional support will be obvious to the child in the expression of the parents' eyes.

PLACES FOR GOD

Children learn by living and experiencing. Through contact with people and objects, a child creates an image of the world around her. Her picture of the world expands gradually from her home to her neighborhood and on to wider horizons.

Does God have a place in the child's emerging picture of the world? The answer to this questions is largely dependent on parents. Do parents give God a place in the child's daily life? Or do parents present God as someone distant and unreal, perhaps present only at church or, even worse, absent altogether.

Too often a parent thinks that a child's thoughts and conception of God will come automatically. A parent might conclude, "My faith isn't well-formed; best I stay out of this." A child's image of God does not emerge on its own. If a father or mother never speak about God, or if there are no images of God present in the child's life, the child has little or no experience, picture, or language in her with which to construct her understanding of God. But if mother and father talk about God and in other ways make God part of their home, God will become real to the child. Dave and fifteen-month-old Terrell love to go for walks in the park together. Often they'll stop along the way and talk about the beautiful things that God has created.

PICTURES OF GOD

Children should have many opportunities to become acquainted with God so that they receive a rich and varied picture of God that corresponds to the biblical story and God's continuing living presence. Parents can speak about God, that God has created them and the whole world, that God watches over the parent and the child and loves and forgives even when they feel angry or have acted wrongly. Parents can speak about Jesus and what he has done, teaching the child that Jesus has shown God to the world. Families can pray at table and bedtime. Families can sing together and go together to worship services, Bible school, and mission events.

Participating in such activities helps the child become acquainted with God through more than simply an inner picture. God becomes a real, living person who is always near with care and forgiveness.

CAN ONE IMAGINE GOD?

A child might speak about God as a human being, yet think of God as someone greater and different. A child can honestly believe that God lives both in his heart and at the same time is bigger than the house.

Such talk sounds meaningless to an adult. Further thought indicates however, that the child in his own way has grasped something important - that God can be described in imperfect pictures, which, although they seem to be paradoxical to an adult, to the child are an expression of his expanding experience. Adults also use pictures from their own experience to think and talk about God. Who can be sure that adult pictures are always more correct than a child's?

The point is that both adults and children are limited in their relationship to God. Human pictures of God will always fall short. God is greater and different than humans are able to perceive. God is not limited to the conception and thoughts that either children or parents have of God.

If a child is to understand this, he must have the opportunity to discover and experience God as close and real each day. The question is whether or not God is to have a place in the child's world. This is largely dependent on parents daring to give God a place in the parents' and the child's shared world.

QUESTIONS FOR THOUGHT AND DISCUSSION

1. Describe how you thought of God when you were a child. Share these thoughts with another parent you trust. Can you find characteristics that are similar in these conceptions of God? What are the differences between your childhood images of God and your images now as an adult?

2. During research on an adult's childhood ideas of God, one of the participants said: "I thought of God as someone like my mother: safe, good, and powerful, who managed and worked with everything." What consequences do you think arise when children's feelings and thoughts mix up their parents with their picture of God?

3. In this chapter it has been emphasized that parents can show a child love through physical contact, concentrated attention, and eye contact. Why is this necessary?

4. Can parents be certain that their adult images of God are always more correct than a child's? Explain your answer.

CHAPTER NINE

Setting Boundaries

Children need boundaries in order to become independent and interdependent. Through limits and boundaries they learn to build up their own life steering and brake system so that they can eventually control and manage themselves.

Two-year old Bobby is being dressed for the out-of-doors. He dashes out of the room, becomes as slippery as an eel, peels off his jacket, and throws his boots across the floor. He is trying his dad's patience. His dad calls out with more determined voice, finds an arm, and holds him firmly. Bobby slips out of his grasp, throws himself down on the floor and screams. He yells and kicks and seems to be hysterical. Dad is in despair. Is something wrong with Bobby?

Two-year olds are not always cooperative with their own or their parents' daily routines. Bobby has now discovered that he has a will of his own and that he can resist his parent's efforts and demonstrates his resistance in a very determined way.

CONFLICTS

Bobby's desire to dress himself is worthy of parental encouragement. But such attempts at self-care don't always fit into family schedules. In addition, Bobby's skills are not always up to the task. Dad has too little time and Bobby has to get dressed. When he was younger it was easier to direct him in the way his dad wanted him to go. Now he has become stubborn and won't yield even when he doesn't know what he wants. Sometimes the conflict can end in a tantrum and parents have difficulty understanding even what the resistance and tantrum are about.

This is why many parents and child-development specialists have called the two and three-year old period the "age of protest," or the "difficult age." How constructively this phase is managed is dependent largely on parents' ability to cope with such protests.

STRONG WILLS

Parents can observe a child's blossoming will and her need to express her growing independence. When she protests, it means that her need for self-assertion is in a state of fluctuation moving toward the capacities of personal initiative, courage, and determination necessary for independence.

At the same time, the child's demands are increasing. She is learning to sit on her potty, to handle silverware at the table, and not pull out all the books from the bookshelves. In short, she is learning to keep rules and routines. Conflicts are unavoidable as she experiences all the demands and regulations as an interference with her own will.

SELF-CONTROL

The problem is not solved by ceasing to make demands of the child or relenting when the child makes his own demands. On the contrary, children need limits in order to become truly independent. Through limits and boundaries, they construct and strengthen their own life steering and braking system so that they will eventually control and manage themselves.

This does not happen overnight. Rather early in their development one can observe the demands building up in the child herself. Mom and Sally, who is two and a half years old, are in the kitchen making an ice cream soda. When Mom answers the telephone in another room, Sally decides to go ahead on her own. The moment she picks up the carton of soft ice cream, she remembers the instruction: "Don't touch the ice cream." She experiences a conflict between "I will" and "Don't." When Mom returns, Sally, with great satisfaction, drops the ice cream on the floor, saying, "No, no, no - don't - no, no, no!"

Sally is experiencing an inner conflict between exercising her own will and the demands from her surroundings. This is progress even though she solves the conflict with a compromise that cannot be accepted. There is still some distance to go until her control system is fully mobilized.

CONSCIENCE

It is too early to speak about conscience. When mom leaves the room, she takes Sally's restrictions with her. Toddlers early on feel guilt when they have done something they shouldn't, but the guilt comes only after the deed is discovered. Only when mom returns and finds the melting ice cream on the floor, does guilt become a factor. It will take more time before the outer authority has moved inward and become part of the child's conscience.

This does not happen automatically. If the child is to develop a conscience and self-control, parents will have to continue to establish boundaries and limits.

BOUNDARIES GIVE SECURITY

Boundaries and limits might create conflicts but must be set. Rules and routines within which the child is free to move are necessary so that a child feels secure as he moves freely within the established limits. Boundaries are also a signal to the child that his parents care about him. These will vary from family to family. Parents have different levels of tolerance for conflicts and tantrums. Parents must set the limits in relation to their own level of tolerance. Once parental boundaries are established, they should be consistently respected by all concerned. If a boundary stretches in all directions like a rubber band there is little stability to give protection and security.

Consistent boundaries and limits presume that parents know why they are establishing them. Thus they become easier to explain to the child. The purpose for the restriction is to assist the child in internalizing the boundary as a part of his framework for life.

On the other hand, it doesn't help to explain to the toddler what he can and cannot do and not follow through. Words and actions must be related. Again and again, parents will be required to lead by the hand, hold, or hinder a child at the same time as they explain and direct.

To make rules become a part of the child's life requires time and patience. When a two year old for the tenth time bites or hits a little brother or sister, it is tempting to let him taste his own medicine. But then he learns that if parents hit someone smaller, he too can hit someone smaller just as he has been doing with his sister. A toddler's security is dependent on a consistent parental stance. However, a child does not need hands that slap. The child needs boundaries, but doesn't need them pounded into him.

TEMPER TANTRUMS

Collisions between a child's willfulness and her boundaries lead often to wild temper tantrums. This happens on occasion with most children of this age. Once her temper is set off, there is very little a toddler can do to control the explosion. Children at this age are without self-control and are, themselves, frightened of the feelings they are unable to master. The howls can go on so long that she loses her breath, her face turns gray, and she almost loses consciousness. Even though it is frightening to watch, the body's natural reflexes will force air into her lungs again.

RESPONDING TO TEMPER TANTRUMS

1. Tantrums often can be prevented. Avoid unnecessary hindrances, prohibitions, irritations, impossible tasks, meaningless orders, nagging, and abrupt disruption of the child's play and plans. (Five-minute warnings of a change often will avoid a clash of wills.) Parents should avoid making demands and orders (such as forcing a child to eat, or to go bed when he is irritable or angry) when there is little chance that they can be carried out. "You're going to whether you want to or not!" is a primitive display of power that very seldom wins, unleashing instead more anger and protest.

2. Do not leave a child who is in the middle of a tantrum. This is a time when he needs protection so he won't hurt himself or someone else. If he begins to hit a sibling or parent, he wants to be stopped because he is unable to stop himself. He is actually anxious about his own anger and is relieved when he is gently stopped.

3. Try not to discuss the situation or punish. During a tantrum, the child is not receptive to reason. Screaming at the child is not constructive; it only strengthens and lengthens the tantrum.

4. Let the child wear out his own tantrum and live through his unpleasant and negative feelings. When he emerges on the other side of the tantrum, he will be both tired and sorry and needs comforting.

5. His tantrum must not be rewarded by relenting and letting him have his way. If this happens, he learns very quickly that tantrums are to be used to his advantage, and they become a means of controlling others. Such use of tantrums must be resisted as far as possible. Instead, parents should let a child experience that such tantrums can isolate him and cut him off from ongoing activities and relationships.

6. It is best to not let fear of what others will say determine the way parents will react. Tantrums in the supermarket, for example, can

be frightfully embarrassing. Parents are sometimes tempted to do anything to stop a tantrum that takes place in a public arena; it is better, as quickly as possible to the take the child away and let him wear out his tantrum in the car.

PARENTAL VALUES

It helps little to react to a child's anger out of one's own anger. Anger is infectious. Parents should develop their capacity to control their own anger, because a child most often responds to what her parents do rather than to what her parents say. Consider the mixed message given when a parent hits a child and says, "Quit hitting!"

Controlling one's anger is naturally more easily said than done. It is not possible, nor is it desirable, never to react with anger. It is no favor to a child to pretend that adults are never angry. Expression of anger from parents need not be destructively directed at a child so that the child's security is threatened. If parents take responsibility for their powerful feelings and direct their power away from the child, the expression of anger can, on the other hand, sometimes clear the air. Reacting to a child's misbehavior with, "When you throw your food, I get angry" is more appropriate than, "If you keep throwing your food, I won't love you."

When parents step over boundaries, they have a great opportunity not only to seek reconciliation, but also to teach good behavior by taking initiative and asking a child's forgiveness. It can be humiliating and difficult; it can also mean much to the child's confidence in her parents and her understanding of God.

QUESTIONS FOR THOUGHT AND DISCUSSION

1. Re-read the story of two-year old Bobby on page 83. Is this a familiar situation in your household? Identify similar examples from your own life and think of positive ways to respond to such situations.

2. What does it mean to say a child needs boundaries and limits in order to feel secure and independent?

3. Some say parents should never reveal anger before their children. What do you think?

CHAPTER TEN

Families - Cradles of Personalities & Character

Families are primary crucibles of humanness. Families are the cradles of personality and character. Whatever happens – or does not happen – in families has fundamental significance for the child all her life.

PARENTS: FILTERS AND LENSES

From the earliest days of a child's life, parents are concerned about the quality of food their child consumes. Parents choose healthy food and nourishing meals and are careful to discern that the child receives nothing that can harm him. Parents function as a filter for their child.

Parents also seek to filter the information and messages a child will receive. Influences that come to the child's early experience are largely controlled by parental choices. This is not only true of parents' conscious stimulation of a child, it also occurs through the influence parents' way of living has on a child.

Families are the interpretive bridge between the child and the world. When a child is young, it is parents who largely determine which television programs their child will watch, if he will attend kindergarten, Sunday school, etc. Parents decide also to a large extent the contact their child will have with other adults and children.

As a child grows older, parents no longer have as much ability to filter their children's contacts with the outside world. During these years, the early experiences of the child within the family will continue to influence their consciousness and decisions. Past experiences within the family become primary glasses through which children view and interpret the world. What children encounter in the larger world, is understood in the light of experiences within the family.

FAMILY VISIONS AND EXPECTATIONS

Given that families are the fundamental influencing factor in a child's early life, what do parents want their family and home life to be? What primary influences do parents want in their child's life? What kind of filters or lenses do parents wish for their child? The answers to these questions are determined by a parent's visions and expectations, which become inherent family filters and lenses. Therefore, it is important that parents think through who they are, what they stand for, and what they intend to accomplish in bringing up their child.

The challenge facing parents is to create a family milieu where a child can have diverse experiences and adventures through play, work, reading, song, music, and trips that best transmit a family's faith, values, expectations, and hopes for the future. In such an environment, the child has the opportunity of developing her own abilities and talents within a safe, meaningful, and hopeful framework!

DAILY INTERACTION - THE LABORATORY OF LIFE

A significant part of this framework will be created by the interaction between the parents themselves. Their relationship as a married couple or as co-parents is important for how well they can function as parents and as persons directly involved in their child's development. When couples and parents set aside time and attention for themselves and each other, the investment also serves their child.

Single parents especially need the friendship and support of other adults. Grandparents and other relatives as well as neighbors and friends become especially important partners in supplying the support that both single and dual parents need in carrying out their responsibilities for a child.

The quality of family life as the milieu for a child's growth is determined by the interaction between adults in the family, between parent and child, as well as between the child and his siblings. Children need adults who are available and who are sensitive to their signals and needs in whatever form and time they are expressed.

In contemporary, post-modern society, opportunities, skills, and time for developing and maintaining such quality of life in families are in short supply. Consequently, now, as never before, families must be open to contact with other children and adults within and without the home who can be partners and resources in creating a solid, resilient, and relationally good community in which children can thrive.

AN OPEN HOME – FORMING A LIFE-GIVING COMMUNITY

Parents and children live in a restless and often impersonal world in which the family can function as a refuge where people can gather for human closeness and warmth. But, if a family withdraws too severely from others and becomes isolated, the emotional pressure on family members can become too great and lead to conflicts and disharmony that will threaten the family.

A home that is open to other significant persons is a safeguard against such distortion and dysfunction. An open hearth tradition will strengthen a family by providing an atmosphere and environment that will increase a child's capacity for friendship, provide parental contact with their child's friends, and enrich the parents' relationship with their own child.

This family openness is not always easy to practice. During the course of a stressful workday, home is often the place where family members look to relax and be themselves. In the evening or on the weekend, it is therefore important to find a balance between the need to include others in both the parents' and child's lives and develop time for individual and parent-child interaction. Intentionality (i.e., thoughtful identification of needs, shared time, and resources) is the key to this balance.

CONGREGATIONS - GOD'S FAITH COMMUNITIES

Congregations are a fine resource for families seeking to open their homes beyond their four walls. The church has many ministries through which both parents and children can find spiritual, moral, and social companionship and mentoring. Many parents have good memories from their own childhood in a faith environment and will want these same good experiences for their own children. Parents should look to the church to receive help in giving their children education and training in the faith in which their children were baptized.

In spite of parents' desire to have their children experience this faith environment, it is sometimes difficult to get families involved in the life of a congregation due to life's fast-pace and constant demands. But the value of parents and children sharing worship, fellowship, and education cannot be overrated. Good relationships and habits that will last throughout their lives will be established. In the midst of this participation children can learn that worship services are an important time for the whole family to be together and focus attention on one's relationship to God.

In addition when families gather to worship together, they show each other that the Christian congregation is a public expression of the family of God. Individual families find a place in the larger fellowship of faith, where the generations can assist and support each other across family boundaries. Such participation in a faith community can also be an antidote to family egoism and isolation.

Such engagement and connection of a family with a faith community does not occur without intentional, concerted effort on the part of the family and congregation. Children often find church services boring and foreign. Parents should not hesitate to work toward gearing worship services and other ministries in the congregation for children. Children are members of the church and have their natural place in the congregation as do adult members. Children, their presence and personalities, their questions and comments, are colorful influences in the life that God has intended for all people.

QUESTIONS FOR THOUGHT AND DISCUSSION

1. Think back to your own childhood family. What are the positive impressions you want to bring into your present family? What do you want your children to remember from their childhood?

2. How do you set aside time and pay attention to yourself and your children's other parent as a component of and contribution to your children's growth?

3. How can your home and family be open to the necessary and enriching resources in the community?

4. When you think about a congregation as an expression of the people of God, do you visualize your own congregation as a community where families are welcome? What can be done in your congregation so that it can function better for both children and adults?

CHAPTER ELEVEN

When Children Ask Questions

"Why is that truck so big, Mom?"

"Who made the wind?"

"Why does Grandpa have such a big nose?"

"Will my teddy bear go to heaven?"

Children ask so many questions. They can literally ask about everything in heaven and earth.

In their first questioning phase, children are more interested in learning what things are called. Then come questions about what people and things are doing. Around the age of four, "why" questions soon begin to badger busy parents.

Not all children ask as many questions as others, and the intensity and content of questions may vary from child to child. Some children are unrelenting with their questions. They can go on without ceasing the whole day, and each answer they receive is a springboard for more questions. Other children are more introverted ponderers and often observe the world with big, wondering eyes. Behind all the variation of questions and curiosity, there are at least two fundamental needs: the need for knowledge and the need for companionship or intimacy.

There is always a reason for a child's questions, even though the reason may not always be obvious. It is logical to interpret the questioning as a child's search for knowledge, when she, in fact, may be asking because she wants companionship. Putting forth a question is one of the many ways children make contact and gain attention.

It is, therefore, important that parents understand what the child is seeking with her questions. If she wants attention, then the words in a parent's answer might be inconsequential. The parent's answer might better come in the contact and closeness through playing, reading a book, or holding the child.

Children's questions can also have an emotional origin. When a child asks why trucks are so big, perhaps the best answer is not that the truck is big because it is needed to transport sand to a construction site; the child may be asking because he is afraid of such a big vehicle. In that case, what he needs is reassurance of his safety and security.

A CHILD'S SEARCH FOR MEANING

Children ask first and foremost because they really want to know. Children have an insatiable need to understand and order their experience in the world about them. Their questions mirror their particular way of thinking. They think that everything is like they are. The teddy bear can think like they do; trees sleep at night; stones hurt themselves when they roll down the mountainside. Children also believe that someone has made everything they see, hear, and feel. "Who made the wind, Daddy?" a child may ask.

In his wonder over how everything came to be, he will ask how he came to be. Soon he will be asking about death, war, hunger, and need in the world. The child begins to marvel over all the big and difficult questions of life. Life is unfolding before him, through experiences within the family and its surroundings, encounters with sickness and death, and through the information a child receives through television.

When children begin their endless why questions, they are not necessarily asking for a reasonable explanation. "Why is it snowing?" a four-year old might ask. To increase the child's knowledge, a parent may explain the freezing point, crystallization, etc. The child however, may be more interested in hearing that it snows so that the trees will be pretty in winter and that children can ride their sleds down the hill. Children are not always after a scientific reason for what happens, but rather are asking for friendly conversation that relates what is occurring to their experience.

FANTASY AND REALITY

Young children often mix reality and fantasy in a way that is difficult for adults to understand. For three and four year olds, dreams are life and life is full of dreams. This is obvious in a child's questions.

A two-year old may run into the living room and ask his father, "Will the bear eat me?" At first, his father doesn't know what the child is talking about; but the father soon learns that his son is afraid to go into his room again. The bear is lying under his bed! It is only when dad goes with the child into the room and they investigate under the bed together, that the child feels safe.

ENGAGING CHILDREN'S QUESTIONS

A parent's attitude toward a child's questions should always give the impression that the questions are important and the answers are designed to engage the child's thoughts, feelings and needs. Parents have a good reason for taking a child's questions seriously, even if the questions seem strange and difficult to understand.

When Whitney asks if God is bigger than the house or stronger than Superman, her parents can't help but smile. But the question indicates that the child is discovering something important about God - that God is bigger and stronger than everyone else. The same is true when a child asks if she can take her favorite toy to heaven with her. In such a question, the child is on the threshold of grasping some of the most important truths about a life of faith - that heaven is a good place to be.

If parents are to know what their child wants with her questions, it means that they will have to listen closely and often encourage the child with another question. "That is a really good question. Do you want to be with your teddy bear in heaven?" The responding question can become the basis for an interesting, satisfying conversation between parent and child.

A child has the right to an honest answer. This does not mean that a parent should always answer to the full extent of her knowledge. "Why do babies come from Mommy's stomach, Daddy?" asks a four-year old. "It's because that's the best place to keep a baby safe," answers Daddy. The answer is short, but true and honest - as far as it goes. In this particular instance, the young questioner is satisfied. It is enough. Later other questions will arise. "Can't Daddy have babies in his stomach, too?" "How do the babies get into mommy's stomach?" These questions can be answered in their own time.

In a parent's answers it is not always the words themselves that are the most important. The words are in many ways transparent. What a child sees behind the words is the interest, the openness, and simplicity that express a parent's attitude and love.

Sometimes parents will have to admit that they don't know the answer to a question. The answer, "I don't know" can be given in many ways, however. It can be said with an attitude of dismissal and impatience. This teaches the child that it was a dumb question -- that the child is not important and the she had better not ask it again. At the worst, the child will avoid questioning the parent. On the other hand, the answer can be given with careful attention and thought, with a commitment to search with the child for the answer -- a clear signal that the question is worth an answer, that the child is important and her question is something that parent and child can solve together.

WONDERING TOGETHER

To take a child's question seriously does not mean that a parent must always give him a full answer or give him the impression that parents know all the answers. This is particularly important when children ask difficult questions about life and death, sickness and suffering, God and heaven.

Sometimes it is best if parents take a step backwards and join their child in looking with awe and respect at a question that the parent cannot answer. Before the greatness and holiness of God, parent and child can explore and wonder and worship.

QUESTIONS FOR THOUGHTS AND DISCUSSION

1. Identify some of the questions your child has asked that you have found difficult to answer. What type of response does the child need?

2. A little boy asked his father: "How did I get into mommy's stomach?" His father answers: "You'll learn more about that when you grow older." What do you think of this answer? Develop other possible answers.

3. It has been said that parents and teachers are often too busy to give children good answers to their questions, so there is little opportunity for a child to explore her natural wonder of the world. It has also been said that a child should have answers to their questions so that they have something about which to marvel. What do you think of these statements? Can these two ideas be integrated?

4. Develop the guidelines for how parents should respond when a child asks questions.

Jesus,

You came from God,

You were a child.

You played as children
*   in Nazareth played.*

You knew what they knew,
*   when they met each*
*   other in the mornings.*

You learned what they built
*   in the sand,*
*   what they made with clay,*
*   and what they did with*
*   sticks and small stones,*
*   what they played when*
*   they chased each other,*
*   and which stories*
*   they heard in the evenings*
*   when it became dark.*

Was that why you were a child, Jesus,
*   because you wanted to learn*
*   how other people played,*
*   know how they laughed,*
*   how they cried,*
*   how it was to be a child*
*   in the human world?*

by Eyvind Skeie

CHAPTER TWELVE
Adult Models

To mature is to grow into the society and culture in which a child is born and makes her way.

A child's journey into mature adulthood is a long process that extends throughout the life of every human being. The journey begins before birth, and the first years of a child's life will have fundamental influence on how she will fit into the society and culture to which she belongs.

There is so much to learn in this process! One rarely consciously remembers the many lessons learned before attending school! It is unbelievable how much a child will acquire during these first six years. A child masters a language during the first four or five years of her life. In addition, foundational attitudes, norms, and values are laid during these years.

LEARNING THROUGH PEOPLE

Most of a child's early learning goes on without the child or parents being aware of it. A child does not learn language, attitudes, and cultural norms within the social structure through theoretical instruction and scheduled training. The first meeting with such values comes through the people in his life—through what they say and do, their habits, practices, and attitudes. A child's immediate family, other relatives, and friends have concrete ways in which they carry on their lives, which establish many of the child's basic norms.

Parents are the child's first models. The child learns by imitating his parents, especially certain physical activities. One can watch a small child literally walk in his father's or mother's footsteps. If one watches closely, it is not only the way parents walk that the child will imitate. Parents can quickly recognize their bodily attitudes, arm movements, favorite expressions, and even their way of speaking emerging in the child. It is almost like seeing oneself in miniature.

A child will not only assume the outer signs of a parent's personality. The imitation goes deeper than that. A child will identify with a parent and will begin to be part owner of a parent's joys and disappointments. He will assume his parents' viewpoints and evaluations and make them his own. Through identification with a definite person such as a parent, the child develops many of his basic attitudes, norms and values. How many parents haven't been embarrassed at one time or another by hearing their child innocently announce to their guests something similar to, "Aunt Lou wears too much makeup!"

OBSERVATION, EXPERIENCE, AND INTERPRETATION

This assimilation does not mean that a child is a passive victim of influences around her. Even though she imitates the adults around her, she is not a carbon copy of her parents' attitudes and actions. For example one can see this as a child learns language. She will learn words and expressions, but will use them according to her own logical sense.

Children interpret and adapt expressions in their own special ways. They are also creators of their own understanding of themselves and their surroundings. Children will not imitate everything and everyone, but choose the models they wish to imitate.

It is difficult to explain why children take after one model and not another. The most important thing for parents to remember is they are their children's first and closest training models, which points to the importance of a parent's great influence of and responsibility to their children.

PARENTAL SELF-REARING

The power of example is a fundamental principle in child rearing. It has been said: "Children are not especially good about listening to adults, but they have always imitated them." This can become cause for parental concern, but should not lead to artificial preaching to a child. Parents sometimes say: "Don't do what I do, do what I say." However, if this becomes a familiar refrain to the child, parents lose their credibility. Children very quickly see through parental ploys and lack of integrity.

Parents must be themselves. However, child rearing challenges parents to become mature. Parents must face the fact that they must sometimes change themselves and their lifestyle -- out of consideration for the child as well as their own sakes. This leads to a type of parental self-rearing.

It is important that parents admit when they've made a mistake. When parents acknowledge that they have fallen short, they are still models. Children who have experienced parents who ask for forgiveness, have learned something that can never be learned through parental warnings or orders.

OTHER ADULT MODELS

In time a child will follow other models. It will not be long before persons and figures on television, as well as in books and magazines become important models and ideals. Television personalities, characters in books, and kindergarten teachers gradually take parents places and models.

However, parents remain the primary models in a child's early life. Parents also have considerable control over the models to which the child will be exposed. Along the way, parents can also help a child form ideas and evaluate impression of their models by talking over what they see and experience in persons whom both the child and parents admire.

BIBLE CHARACTERS

The Bible is filled with stories about people who can be models both for children and adults. These Bible characters are models, not because they are glossy pictures of perfect people—on the contrary, they are people of God who have made mistakes, as well as struggle with God and each other. What's most important about these models is that they teach both parents and children about God's relationship with them and their place in God's mission in the world.

Stories about Moses, Abraham, Joseph, and many other Old Testament characters are not only dramatic and exciting, they provide the opportunity for a child to identify with that person's battles, defeats, and triumphs. A child gains the assurance that God can be experienced by real people. God can be experienced as someone with whom a child can talk and in whom the child can have confidence.

It is the same with the disciples and other personalities a child meets in the New Testament. When children identify with these biblical characters, they see Jesus through the biblical character's eyes and experience. In this process children become acquainted with Jesus as a person who is present with them as a friend who is close by.

GROWING UP WITH CHRIST

Bible characters show a child humankind can be both good and bad. Through Jesus, a child comes face to face with the love and goodness of God made manifest in flesh and blood. Christ's life presents both children and adults with an impulse and challenge to live truthfully and honestly. In bringing up a child there is great value in showing him there is a person who never leaves him nor rejects him.

Children discover quickly that parents and other models can be disappointing, even as children disappoint themselves. Both parents and children can present themselves to Jesus Christ who is more than a model. He is a Savior and Lord who forgives and provides new beginnings.

QUESTIONS FOR THOUGHT AND DISCUSSION

1. It is important that parents know beyond a shadow of a doubt that they function as models for their child. In what ways are you a good model, and in what areas are you not? How are you a positive or a negative model for your child?

2. Parents are models for their children as to what it means to be a boy or girl, a man or woman. What is your child learning from you about sex roles and sexual identification?

3. Some children grow up without a father in their home; many out-of-home caregivers are women. What significance do you think this has for a particular child's development?

4. Many of the characters in the Bible are far from good ethical models. In what ways can parents use the stories about these people as learning experiences for their child?

PART FOUR:
Young Children

CHAPTER THIRTEEN
Threat and Security

*Security is the foundation for child-rearing.
If children are to experience healthy
development and to learn well, they
must feel secure.*

EXPANDING A CHILD'S SECURITY

During the months of infancy and the life of a toddler, a parent's
task is to give a child confidence in her immediate surroundings and
in herself. This is necessary so that the child can begin exploring her
world. During her third and fourth years a child can move into
larger arenas of life and expand her exploration.

If the child is to feel brave enough to dare further adventure, her
sense of security must also be extended. Her boundaries may have
expanded to include the sandbox and neighborhood playground;
therefore, she now requires the inner security to explore the broad-
ened horizons that have taken her outside her own home.
Throughout her life, there will be a connection between that which
gives security and her courage in risking more expansive exploration.

DEVELOPING A YOUNG CHILD'S CAPACITY TO COPE

1) Love your child—regardless

Children are not always loveable. What happens to a parent's love when the child whines, tries his parent's patience or misbehaves badly is critical in expanding security during these early childhood years. Parents cannot, of course, accept everything a child does. On the contrary, parental love for a child commits them to correction and setting limits. Sometimes the way parents fulfill this obligation might make a child feel his parents have withdrawn their love. At that moment, the parents themselves might feel that way as well!

These are natural feelings, however, parents should not use their love as a weapon to keep a child in line. Actions, even words that tell the child, "If you don't behave, Mommy and Daddy won't love you anymore," destroy a child's self worth and security. Children should not be taught that love is dependent on proper behavior. Genuine love can not be bought, it can only be given freely.

When parental love has been violated or misused, forgiveness can restore the broken relationship. When children and parents can ask each other for forgiveness, security is strengthened. If children experience forgiveness with accountability, they will be able to better understand the Christian message of God's unconditional love and forgiveness.

Children ask often, more through body language than with words, "Do you love me?" A child's feelings of security are dependent on a positive answer to this spoken or unspoken question, regardless of how he behaves or misbehaves. This unconditional love is shared with a child by giving him frequent, good physical contact and concentrated attention. Eye contact, holding his hand, patting or rubbing his back, as well as comforting and holding him when he is frightened or hurt are all examples of good, physical contact.

Concentrated attention happens when parents listen carefully to their child as he tells them something. It is important for parents to take time to engage a child when he shows them a drawing or project in which he is pleased. All of this builds confidence that he is appreciated and loved.

2) Boundaries and consistency

A child's feeling of safety is dependent on rules regarding what she can and cannot do. These rules should be consistently followed and even-handedly enforced. A young girl is confused and unsure if her mother says "yes" and her father says "no," or if a rule is not followed in practice.

A "no" can mean disappointment, of course, but a child can be helped to overcome her disappointment. One of the ways to help her overcome the disappointment is to explain to her the reason for the "no" and then provide other acceptable options.

When parents set limits and boundaries, it is not only to provide security for the child during the early years. As the child grows, she must begin to establish her own boundaries. Parents cannot always walk beside a child and take care of her. As she grows, the child will have to establish her own boundaries and discipline herself to live within them. Inner control is built up as the child gradually takes responsibility for herself. It begins with small things, such as choices regarding toys or clothes or furniture in her room. When a child chooses for herself, she builds up trust in herself.

3) Consistent values and rules create security

Small children like routine and rituals! They appreciate doing things like they were done before. Routines and rituals enable children to understand a situation and master it, which in turn add to their feelings of safety.

Each family must find its own values and rules within which the child can move freely as the whole family orders its day-to-day life, weekly rhythms, traditions and holidays. Family members often are busy, each doing his/her own thing. Establishing schedules becomes more difficult as the number of activities grows. How often the family is together is not as important as establishing key times for connecting, times that the family really is together. It can be at breakfast or dinner each day, or bedtime, or car time, attendance at church, a family game evening, a special Saturday activity, or Sunday outings.

Most parents establish a regular bedtime ritual. This gives the child a feeling of security. It is a good time to talk with one another about experiences both parents and the child had throughout the day. While it is better if this time with the child is longer rather than shorter, it is the quality of that time that matters the most. The key quality of these times is concentrated attention.

Evening prayers as a conclusion to the day contribute to a child's security and more. When parents pray with a child, they teach a child that God is a person to whom one can speak and in whom the child can have confidence. When parents and children talk with God, God becomes a living person and teaches a process that establishes basic content and language for use in speaking meaningfully about God. Children who are accustomed to praying to God at home will more easily experience and understand God when they hear about God in Sunday school or worship services.

CHILDHOOD FEARS

Even the child who is very secure experiences situations in which her feelings of safety are threatened. Threats can come from outside the child or they can be brought on from within by something the child has done. Fear, anxiety, and guilt are natural feelings resulting from both personal behavior and perceived external threat.

None of these feelings is harmful in itself, and fear can keep a child from doing something that is dangerous. For example, fear of fire can help a child be careful with matches.

It can be painful for both children and parents, however, to experience these feelings. When a child is taken to the doctor for shots, it is tempting for a parent to say, "Don't be afraid. If you don't cry, you'll get a treat." This does not help a child accept the pain and unpleasant feelings as a part of life. It is wiser to acknowledge the fear, consider options for dealing with the fear, and be close by to reassure the child. Fear and guilt can easily take over without real cause. When a child experiences exaggerated feelings of anxiety and guilt, she may be unable to function and experience social growth.

TENDING A CHILD'S FEELINGS AND MOODS

• Adults can do something about the impressions a child receives.

In so far as possible, parents should avoid exposing a child to unnecessary fright and threats. By preparing a child in advance for scary activities such as going to the doctor, parents can avoid letting new and unusual experiences with strangers catch the child unprepared.

• Adults can put words to a child's feelings.

A child must be encouraged to show his feelings and talk about them. Fright becomes even more of a burden if a child is afraid to express his fear. Boys and girls must be allowed to cry. Parents can model this behavior for their child by acknowledging, putting words to, and expressing their own hurt and fear.

• Adults can attack the problems.

Children are capable of mastering their unpleasant feelings. They can work them out through fantasy and play, or they can do something with them directly, such as when a child is allowed to turn on the monster vacuum cleaner. It is important the child learns to master the problem that makes her feel insecure.

When a child feels guilty, the problem is often that she has done something that she knows is outside her boundaries. The sense of guilt is a signal. In this case, it is the guilt that can become the problem. Parents can help a child by identifying what happened, working through the accountability, encouraging forgiveness, and letting the child know she is deeply loved regardless of what she does.

• **Parents can be examples for their child.**

Adult caregiver's feelings, whether positive or negative, are transferred to their child. When security is threatened, everything depends on how the parent responds to the situation. Sometimes just the knowledge that a parent is available is enough to make a child feel safe. Children need constant recharging of the batteries of love and care, of emotional security in their lives. This recharging is necessary for both solving their own problems and in giving love and security to others. A child's love is a thank you for a parent's love!

Because of the constant need for these signs of love, parents also need to find ways to fill up their reservoirs of love over and over again. Parents can not give away that which they haven't received.

QUESTIONS FOR THOUGHT AND DISCUSSION

1. "If you aren't good, then Mommy and Daddy won't love you anymore!" This is, fortunately, a rare statement parents make to their child. But it can also be communicated through a parent's attitude or behavior and leave a deep impression on a child. Can you find examples of this in your parenting or caregiving?

2. Identify schedules, routines and rituals that work successfully in creating feelings of security within your family.

3. Parents often comfort children by admonishing them with words such as, "Don't cry!" "Don't be afraid!" How might parents assist a child to express his unpleasant feelings?

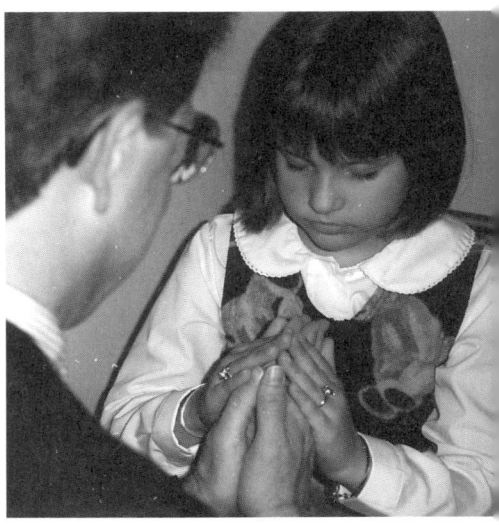

CHAPTER FOURTEEN

Conscience and Forgiveness

Teaching children what is right and wrong is at the heart of child rearing. However, it is not always easy to know what a parent should do when a child has done something wrong.

Words such as discipline, obedience, and guilt often have negative connotations in post-modern society. This is not without cause. These notions have often been mixed with brute force and blind obedience. However, parents cannot dismiss the importance of discipline, obedience, and acknowledgment of guilt in a child's life. These dynamics are necessary for a child to become an independent and responsible person.

CONSCIENCE

When a child is two or three, she has not developed much of a conscience. For toddlers, boundaries and norms are usually what is allowed or not allowed by parents repeatedly giving orders to the child. The child is completely dependent on having a parent near by to watch her. She does not understand that she has done something wrong before she is discovered and perhaps punished. Gradually however, parents will notice that this outer control begins to move into the child's consciousness.

One notices this when a child talks to a doll, an action figure, an imaginary playmate, or a younger sibling. Parents often hear their own words when the child says, "Now, be good!" "Don't touch that!" "Watch out!"

After a time a parent will hear the child saying the same things to herself. In the beginning, the admonition to herself comes after the action. She kicks a ball into the flowerbed, and immediately after says, "Don't kick the ball into the flowers!" Later she begins to warn herself before the action. "Not in the flowers!" As if a parent had said it to her, she turns and kicks the ball in another direction.

CHILDREN IMITATE ADULTS - THE POWER OF EXAMPLE

Children model their parents and other people who are close to them. They become as one with them; they identify with them. A three-year-old boy awakens at six in the morning and begins to make noise. His drowsy father stumbles into his room and in a stern voice, commands him to go back to bed and stay there until seven. The little boy complies and becomes quiet. But very soon the father hears noises from the boy's room again. He lies in bed, as he had been told to do, but he suddenly sticks an arm over the edge of the bed, draws it back under the covers saying, "Get into bed!" Then a foot finds its way out of the covers and is chided immediately. "You heard what I said!" comes from his room, and the foot is tucked under the covers again. At last, he moves closer to the edge of the bed, then rolls back to the middle, and commands in stern voice, "And stay there until seven!"

What happens is that the young boy assumes his father's role and uses it as a means to command himself. The father moves, in a manner of speaking, into the child with his norms and authority. The father's spoken commands are becoming inner commands and part of the child's self-control mechanism. His father's voice is becoming a part of his own conscience. In the forming of an inner conscience, parents have a cooperative partner in their own child. It will take many years, however, before this partner is able to take over the whole task. When a child time after time is faced with using rules and norms in practice, his conscience is forming within his developing a life-coping system.

This happens from the very beginning as the child learns what is acceptable and not acceptable. Eventually the child must learn to commit himself to that which is acceptable. Then he is ready to exercise his built-in conscience that will tell him when he is performing an acceptable or unacceptable deed.

Children are exposed to norms and values through the atmosphere in a family, through what parents say and even more so through what parents do. Research supports over and over again the old rule of the power of example. The most effective method of teaching a child right from wrong is through parental modeling and example. Children are better at imitating adults than at listening to them! To bring up a child is a challenge for parents because in so doing parents are bringing up themselves. Parents are challenged by their child to change those aspects of their lives that they know hinder their own growth and which do not set a good example for their children.

This does not mean that parents pretend to be perfect. If parents say one thing and live another, children will play at integrity as well. Children need parents who are honest and genuine and define themselves by living out their own convictions. Good parental models behave before a child the same as they behave with others. Parents cannot expect children to be more polite and considerate than they are themselves. Thoughtful behavior is infectious.

When parents are in a position to lead a child, they should do so positively. It is better to say, "Do this," instead of, "Don't do that." And when a child asks why, she will be no wiser if a parent responds with "because I say so!" The explanation should be reasonable

enough so that it will help the child when she is in the same situation again. The goal is for the child to do the right thing because
she is convinced of it through understanding.

GUILT FEELINGS

A child needs praise and encouragement in order to do what is right
or good. When he does wrong, parents can use their skills to help
him understand why what he did was wrong. Guilt feelings play an
important role and are healthy in these situations. It is a good sign
when a child feels guilty when he has done something wrong. It
shows that his conscience is coming to life and doing its work. It is
best not to smooth over these feelings as if they don't really matter,
for such an attitude indicates to the child that his parents do not
take him seriously. If a brother, while in a temper tantrum, destroys
his sister's block construction, his resulting feelings of guilt are a
healthy sign. Parents might take advantage of the situation to discuss
the actions that gave rise to the feelings. Keep the discussion at a
level the child can comprehend and include understanding, forgiveness, and accountability.

Sometimes children experience unhealthy guilt feelings that seem to
have no definite cause, seem implausible and persist. If a child hangs
on to feelings of guilt in spite of being assured that he is forgiven, it
is a sign that the guilt is tangled in an unhealthy way with something
else. This is especially true if the child is consistently afraid of doing
something because he fears he might do something wrong and loses
his spirit of adventure. In the most severe cases, parents may need
to seek help from a pediatrician or child counselor.

FORGIVENESS

Forgiveness with accountability is a critical component of child rearing. When a child honestly confronts her wrong-doing, experiences
sorrow for the difficulty caused by her actions, and is forgiven, usually her feelings of guilt are gone. Then a child can start fresh with
herself and others.

Living with a burden of guilt for which she has not received forgiveness is damaging to the development of a child's personality and confidence. Forgiveness gives a child new power and courage. That which created pain for the child and those she has hurt has been taken up honestly in their relationship, dealt with, and now she can look forward to new experiences with confidence and greater security.

A parent's responsibility is to create a safe atmosphere in which children dare to confess a wrong committed and ask for forgiveness. Such an atmosphere is characterized by openness, mutual forgiveness, and acceptance. In this graceful atmosphere, children feel truly forgiven and learn to forgive others. Once more, the example of parents and other adults can have a positive impact within a healed relationship. Children who have parents who forgive and who ask for forgiveness themselves, have developed a fundamental character building-block that will serve them well in their own parenting.

At the moment of forgiveness, parents and children often experience more than human love in action; in these times, both parents and children can turn to God for encouragement and healing.

"FORGIVE US OUR TRESPASSES"

In what Christians know as The Lord's Prayer, Jesus taught both adults and children to ask for forgiveness. They are invited to do so by the One sent from God to express God's unconditional love. Sometimes it is good for parents to make this forgiveness of God very specific by making a list of those things for which the parent needs forgiveness. In this process both parent and child experience forgiveness concretely. In such an exercise in faith, it is important for a parent to celebrate in the presence of the child the grace of God that gives the parent courage to confess, the accountability of making restitution, and the joy of feeling unburdened and free of guilt.

QUESTIONS FOR THOUGHT AND DISCUSSION

1. Some parents are convinced that a child should not experience feelings of guilt. Do you agree? Can you distinguish between healthy and unhealthy feelings of guilt?

2. Can you remember a time when you were a child and an adult asked you for forgiveness? If so, how did you experience this request? What do you think it means to a child when she witnesses her parents asking each other for forgiveness?

3. How do you respond to your child when he comes to you and confesses that he has made a mistake or done something wrong?

Two Crabs

An old crab and her offspring

wandered the sandy bottom of the

sea, sideways and backwards,

they moved.

"You're walking crookedly!" said

the mother to her offspring.

"You must walk gracefully, and

straight forwardly."

"I will," replied her offspring,

"if only you'll go before me and

show me the way."

Aesop

CHAPTER FIFTEEN

Impulses and Self-Expression

Parents are eager for their children to develop their talents and interests. How do parents best encourage their children? When does encouragement become manipulation or worse, vicarious satisfaction of a parent's frustrated dreams?

A CHILD'S GROWTH AND ADULT ENCOURAGEMENT

It is important to find a good match between a child's inner growth and her external influences. God has given each child inherent abilities. Parents must be on the lookout for opportunities through which their child can discover and practice her talents and experience the pleasure of competency. Children should be encouraged to explore their emerging impulses and be exposed to opportunities for development in many and varied areas, e.g. art, sports, creative crafts, drama, music, etc. A child's abilities and interests do not develop automatically. When parents say that a child is musical, it probably means that she has been exposed to the world of music through singing, playing an instrument, or listening to music and has shown promise.

Parents, however, can be too eager to push their child, especially in the areas in which parents have interest and competency. In so doing, parents can cause undue pressure and frustration for themselves and their child by the unrealistic expectations and demands that are made.

INFORMATION AND IMPULSES

Children develop their abilities in a web of interaction with influences from an ever widening world. Children receive information from their surroundings; in turn, children influence their surroundings as they express their thoughts, feelings, and interests.

Children receive messages as they listen to stories and nursery rhymes, songs, watch television, look at pictures, etc. A child's reflective and creative impulses are expressed in many forms, such as drawing and coloring, modeling with clay, singing, and dancing.

Parents can expand both their child's imagination and intelligence through such activities as intentionally exploring the tasks of daily life, visiting a zoo or library, playing creative games, participating in family rituals, attending Christian worship experiences, and reading to them.

PLAYING AND LEARNING

Small children develop their abilities and interests first and foremost through play. The child who has had the chance to play to his heart's content, has a greater capacity later to use his own creativity and abilities in his career as an adult.

A child's play is not just entertainment. It is also serious work. "Don't bother me, I'm working!" says a four-year old who sits at the table and scribbles on a piece of paper. "We're playing garden," says Bobby who helps his mom with a spade in the backyard.

Children discover themselves through their play. By role playing "mamma-papa-baby," "hospital," "school," "shop," "cars," they learn the functions of key societal roles. In so doing they are testing and developing their own abilities and skills; they are experimenting with their own identity.

THE JOY OF MUSIC AND MOVEMENT

The first musical experience of a child is most likely parents or care-givers humming or singing to the newborn infant in their arms.

Not everyone finds it natural to sing for or with a young child; this is especially true for parents who think they can't sing. It is your voice that your child loves; a quality musical presentation is not the point. By singing to your child, companionship and security are generally deepened and the child is encouraged to sing and be creative.

Young children often respond to music by waving their arms and legs; almost all small children receive pleasure from music. Music is many things to children - songs, rhythmic play, rhymes and jingles, free movement, use of instruments, bells etc. Every child will respond to one or more of these opportunities to make music.

SONGS AND SINGING GAMES

Children of all ages love singing games and find it even more fun when adults join them. Children learn to match their voices with movement and sound through musical games. Songs with texts full of action are popular and children sing them over and over again. They ask again and again for their favorite jingles. They delight in the words and often play with them.

Children have a knack for rhyming the words of songs with words they make up.

Children also like songs and melodies without words. A family can create its own orchestra with simple instruments such as lids, tin cans, drums and sticks, kazoos, and whistles. Even the youngest of children can learn rhythm by clapping her hands. This type of family play is more to a child than the music or noise the family is making together; it is doing a shared activity that develops togetherness and communicates love.

THE CHILD AS ARTIST

Art, like music, gives a child tremendous pleasure and valuable opportunity for self-expression. Children love to draw, color, do cut-outs, and paste using a great variety of materials.

In the beginning the actions of drawing and molding clay are the child's primary goals; gradually the artwork itself becomes important. Drawing and molding clay are a child's expression of herself. At times children find it easier to express their thoughts and experiences through color and clay than through language. When children proudly display their art, most parents wisely take time to look at the work and not only praise their child, but also talk with them about what it means and how the child felt when creating it. Only an unthinking adult would ever try to correct a child's drawing so it would be right. It is important for parents to be open to a child's own method of speaking through her art, using it as a means for understanding what the child is expressing.

OPPORTUNITIES FOR "UNFOLDING"

Children need space and materials for their drawing and molding activities. Newspaper, plastic table clothes, or large sheet-rock panels can be used. A large roll of paper, blackboard and chalk, wooden blocks and boards, clay, paste, scissors, scraps of cloth, colored paper, anything that can be used to good advantage will enable a child's imagination to soar. The most important thing is that the parent and the child feel safe with the arrangement and the busy child can work undeterred.

QUESTIONS FOR THOUGHT AND DISCUSSION

Below are listed three components of a child's development. Indicate your preference in degree of importance for each of the areas in the upbringing of your child.

How much importance do you feel each has?

	Very little	Little	Average	Great
A. Physical activity				
B. New ideas, information, knowledge				
C. Creativity with music/art				

1. If you had to choose, which of these areas would you choose as most important? Why? Would your choices be the same if the child was a girl or a boy?

2. Which roles does your child most enjoy playing? What is the significance of this role-playing in your child's development?

3. Research shows that when small children play outside, they play very close to the entrance to the house. Do you have a place for your child to play close to the entrance to your home? Could you develop one if you don't? How might you improve the one you have?

CHAPTER SIXTEEN

Friends

A child is born for relationships with people. Only through relationships with others can a child develop and become independent and interdependent. It is important for a child to become acquainted with adults and other children -- and from these acquaintances develop significant friendships.

INTERACTION WITH ADULTS

A two or three-year-old's relationship with her parents is strongly influenced by her awakening will and a need for independence. A four year old goes throught periods of tranquility and delight in mastery, only to be followed by times of upheaval and disharmony. The child goes through enormous developmental leaps, preparing to move to the next stage of mastery. At age five, a child may enter a calmer phase. She becomes more cooperative. At this age, she ceases protesting and becomes more amenable to her parents' suggestions. It becomes easier for parents and child to converse, work, and play.

Through the child's interactions during the first four years, she has acquired language. A child's developing language skills become an important tool in her further attachment with other people. Parent and child can converse at significantly more complex and carefully nuanced levels than before. Four and five year olds ask searching questions and will desire reasonable explanations for everything. Children of this age especially like to hear stories about their parents' childhood, delight in simple stories told over and over again by their parents and other adults. Children want to tell their stories too and become more and more enthusiastic when adults are willing to listen.

PLAY AND WORK

Even though children at this age are more skilled at playing alone or with other children, they still enjoy having adults around. They especially enjoy musical and intergenerational circle games that require both singing and movement. Children experience care and security as well as fun and entertainment in these positive moments of togetherness with their family or caregivers.

Playing with children is good for adults as well. These are moments when parents can tap into the memory banks of their childhood. When parents enter a child's world of games, their friendship with the child is developed and strengthened.

It is also important for children to enter their parents' world—both within and outside the home. Four and five-year-olds enjoy helping their parents with activities such as cooking, car washing and gardening. Whether or not their work is done well enough is not the primary objective. It is meaningful for a child simply to be part of the family's work day.

Working together provides parent and child an excellent opportunity for developing their relationship. Parents can coach or assist a child in his work in such a way that the child doesn't feel chided for his clumsy skills or sloppy work. A child needs encouragement for his attempts, which builds up confidence in their abilities.

ARE PARENTS FRIENDS?

Children need adult friends of both sexes and different ages. Parents can be good friends with children even as they retain their executive responsibilities; and young children feel good when their parents are friends with each other. Children delight in seeing their parents play and work together.

What happens when a child's parents quarrel and their parents' friendship disintegrates or their parents divorce? In the worst scenario a child feels he must choose which of the two will be his friend. Often the child believes he is responsible when his parents go separate ways.

This is a difficult situation for a child. It is important for parents to view their situation through the eyes of their child. If their relationship has become too difficult and is fractured, it is a good idea to seek professional help and counseling whether parents are married, separated, or divorced.

GRANDPARENTS, OTHER RELATIVES, AND FRIENDS

Grandparents have excellent opportunities to be good friends and mentors with their grandchildren. When distances are great between grandparents and their grandchildren, creative use of letters, phone calls, e-mail, videotapes, and regular visits can build and sustain significant relationships of support and guidance. Contact with grandparents and older adults provides a child with stories, wisdom, and roots that will enrich her and provide stability all her life.

It is important for children to become acquainted with their uncles and aunts, cousins, and parents of their friends. Adults are role models for children. Experiencing a rich variety of close adults provides children with the breadth of models and mentors needed to expand the child's horizons and imagination of who they might become.

FRIENDSHIP WITH OTHER CHILDREN

Friendship with adults has its unique enriching value for a child. A child's friendship with siblings and peers provides yet another dimension to his development. Through play and comradeship with other children, a child learns to be considerate, to share, and to fit in with others. In these activities with other children, a child establishes the foundation for future cooperation and compatibility in the community.

Children with siblings come by these experiences in their families at an early age. Neighborhood playmates, kindergartens, and day care centers also provide opportunities for establishing these lasting friendships where children can learn acceptable social skills.

Sometimes a child creates an imaginary friend. This can be good when it fills a need, even though an imaginary friend can never take the place of a real one.

As a child grows older, friends become a steadily increasing part of his life which means a child's friends are very important to his parents. Encouraging and guiding their children's friendships is a critical and delicate parental dance of discernment.

Children of this age are learning to play and work well together. However, learning to be cooperative and adjusting to each other does not happen overnight. Often there will be fights over toys, an unwillingness to take turns, and difficulties in sharing.

CONFLICTS

Children not only have conflicts, they can unrelentingly tease and torment each other. Getting through these difficult altercations creatively and wisely is taxing but crucial for both parent and child. Should children learn to stand their ground or return blow for blow? Should they give in? Without knowing the context, an absolute "yes," or "no," to these questions is impossible. These situations can be so difficult for a child that a parent cannot demand that he handle them all in the same way. What's crucial is that as often as possible, parents use these situations to teach children to solve conflicts.

In these teaching-learning moments, parental modeling is crucial as always. How do Mom and Dad respond to one another when they are irritable or have differences? What does Dad do when the neighbors complain that he drives too fast in the neighborhood? Is there respect for everyone in the family when there are conflicts? The family's atmosphere and values around anger and conflict set the stage for the way a child approaches solving conflicts. Children learn both the range of options and the skills of conflict resolution from adults. Children learn more from how parents tackle their own conflicts than from what parents tell them to do in conflict.

In addition, children often watch the way the adults solve conflicts on television. When children have few close adult contacts, they substitute television heroes and heroines; consequently, questionable film characters who most often solve conflicts violently, become their models.

FRIENDS WITH JESUS

Even though God is the awesome maker and maintainer of the universe, God is not an impersonal power far away from God's people. God has come close, concretely in everyday reality through Jesus Christ.

Children are capable of experiencing well-informed beliefs very early in life, through acquaintance with Jesus as their friend. For this to occur, children must first hear about Jesus...about his life, his activities, his friends, and the stories he told.

If children are to become friends with someone, they must have contact with that person, talking with and learning about the other. Jesus seeks to know both parents and children. They can meet him in the Bible and talk with him through songs and prayers. If Jesus has a regular place in conversation and becomes a part of daily family life, children learn that Jesus is truly a friend who is always present, a friend who can be trusted.

QUESTIONS FOR THOUGHT AND DISCUSSION

1. Identify experiences whereby parents can be together with their children working and playing.

2. What opportunities do your children have to get to know their grandparents? How can you encourage these relationships? If your child's grandparents are dead or live too far away for frequent contact, does your child have opportunity to be friends with elders who live close by?

3. Suppose Jonathan is best friends with your little girl, Amy. Each day he sits in the sandbox and waits for her to come out and play. Everyday Amy arrives to play with him. One day when Amy goes to the sandbox, she finds Jonathan playing with Sally. Jonathan and Sally won't let Amy play with them.

   Should Amy's mother intervene? Do you think the children should work this out themselves? If you decide to get involved, how would you go about it? If the situation had been the other way around, so that it was your child who did not want to share her best friend, would you handle the situation differently?

4. What can a parent do so that a child will come to know Jesus as a real and living person? As a friend?

CHAPTER SEVENTEEN

Early Life Experiences and Feelings

Usually ages four and five are a stable period of energy and delight in life.

Children have learned to control the large movements of their arms and legs; they have mastered language; they have explored and learned much of their world. A four-year-old can bubble with the joy of life, and is a joy to himself and others.

A CAREFREE CHILDHOOD?

Engaging the richness of human emotion does not come without care and effort. Children need situations where both good and bad feelings can be experienced and expressed.

When a child enjoys beauty or humor or success, adults find it natural to laugh and share the child's joy with her. It is just as important for a child to express sorrow and for adults to feel sad or weep with her. When sorrow enters a family, parents have a tendency to shelter a child from reality. A happy and harmonious childhood, void of crises, tension, and pain, is not the same as a carefree childhood. What's important for a child is having someone close by who can share her experience during a crisis; it means having a place to go where feelings can have words put to them and where positive, supportive attention can be given to the child and her feelings.

EXPERIENCE CHANGES WORDS INTO REALITY

Many and varied experiences are necessary to help a child change mere words into reality. Concrete relationships, events, and activities help a child transfer theory to reality.

A parent can talk with a child about horses, boats, factories, art, justice, or forgiveness. But if these words are to have any meaning for the child, a parent must also tie them to concrete experiences. When a child has been with his mother to the factory where she works, the word factory then has concrete and meaningful content for him. In like manner only when a child has experienced forgiveness, does he learn what the word means.

The same is true of a child's faith. Parents can talk to children about God. But if the word God is to have meaning and content, the child must experience God as God. Children can experience God both in the domestic church and in the public church. Children can experience God in Bible stories of Jesus, through participation in prayer, caring conversation, serving someone else in Jesus' name, and eventually in Holy Communion. In these activities, God becomes a living, specific reality for the child, a person with whom she can talk, one who forgives her, one with whom she can care for others, and one to whom she can go with her joys and sorrows.

Many parents ask if young children can understand anything of God and faith. The answer is: To understand, a child must experience. If children are to understand anything of Holy Communion, for example, they must be present and participate in Holy Communion. The thought is not enough for a child to understand; in fact, simply learning the content is not the only object; it is important that parents allow a child to receive all the gifts God will give. To receive God's gift of love requires neither understanding, prestige, or power. Parents don't wait to hug a child until the child understands what a hug is! God does not wait to love a child until the child understands what love is!

LIVING AND TENDING EMOTIONS

Children need to identify their experiences concretely. What emotional color might a child ascribe to a particular experience? Is the experience of mother's work in the factory light and happy, or dark and gloomy? Is the child's experience of God one of light and graciousness, or something gray and sad? A child's emotional colors and moods are determined largely by the way parents allow the child to experience and express life's fullness in specific words and actions.

Some parents experience Christianity as anything but a message of good news. In such cases, it is understandable that these parents will keep their children away from church. Such parents might well find a church that values children and at least gives the children a chance to experience God as the One who wants salvation and goodness for parents and their children, who forgives, and redeems and who is ready to give them joy in their lives.

ENJOYING CLOSENESS

How can parents encourage and enrich a child's experience of goodness and joy? For small children, the greatest joy is experiencing something good in the company of their parents.

Most parents find they have too little time to be with their children. If this is the case, it becomes more important to use the time a parent does have with the child very intentionally. A parent can begin by developing reasonable and regular rhythms in her relationship with the child. If a parent doesn't have time until late afternoon to be with the child during work days, the parent can set aside some time on Saturday morning and be faithful and imaginative in planning their conversation and activities. The child will come to trust and value the routine and look forward to it.

Family trips are times to explore new and exciting adventures generating something to remember together with pleasure. The challenge with such times is to find a balance between the often differing needs of parents and children. These outings are valuable even if everyone in the family doesn't get as much out of the experience as others, at least all can have the connection and memory of being together as a family.

READING WITH CHILDREN

One cannot overemphasize the importance of reading to and with children. Children love it! Reading to a child is an experience of companionship and closeness. A child receives nourishment for his thoughts and imagination as well as for his feeling and connectedness with his parents and family. Reading to and with a child offers topics for conversation and impulses for play, drawing, molding with clay, and other creative activities.

Folk tales and stories can be longer and more involved at this age. A little boy or girl can live intensely in imaginary stories. Even though they know the story is not true, their fantasies are a way for them to explore their world.

At this age, a child can become acquainted with the great books of the world to be found in the public library. Children's sections in libraries are usually full of interesting books that allow their imaginations to soar; many librarians hold children's story times in which fascinating new books are read, folk stories told, and puppet shows presented.

Many parents read through a children's Bible story book with their four and five-year-old. This is a great time to explore the great persons, places, and events in the sweep of God's people. Reading through the many stories of God's relationship with the world and God's people gives the parent and child opportunity to find themselves in God's story and speak of their faith with each other.

TELEVISION

For good or ill, television is usually part of a child's life. Television provides opportunities for a child to experience images and words. With her own eyes, she can see huge worlds, both real and imaginary.

For children, images and pictures on television are not always what they appear to be. Children need adults to help interpret what they've viewed. It is important for them to talk about what they have viewed and work through their impressions. It is wise for parents to be close by when they see something frightening appear on the screen.

It is a good idea, therefore, for parents to watch television with their children. By watching television with one's child, one not only has some control over the images engaging a child, but as in reading to a child, the television viewing opens possibilities for shared experiences of curiosity, joy and fun as well as compassion for the needy, suffering, and sorrowing. While watching a television special for children, four-year-old James and his Dad heard about a program to help needy children. Along with Mom, they decided to contribute financially to the program and have continued doing so for fifteen years.

One difficulty with children watching too much television is that there will be little time left for their creative fantasy. A little boy expressed his frustration when he said: "There are better pictures in the radio!" By simply listening, his imagination could be given full play.

THE JOY OF SHARING

The happiness of young children is multiplied when shared with others. In fact, children often teach adults that happiness is meant to be shared. Families can experience pleasure in small everyday occurrences. Adults express their delight and appreciation when a little hand reaches out with a dandelion or a sheet of paper with his latest piece of art. Children can also learn that both parents and children belong to a larger family. In addition to sharing good things in one's own family, parents can lead their children in sharing with needy people in other places of the world. Children can help collect gifts, money, clothing, and toys. Parents and children can rake the yard of a handicapped person. These are wonderful ways by which to experience the joy of sharing. A family's adoption of a child in another part of the world will teach children to love and share themselves with another.

If a family gets new neighbors, the whole family can make contact. Through such personal involvement with their parents, a child's interest and concern will develop into a wider fellowship and the urge to share will become more natural. This is the power of specific, personal experiences. To invite the lonely and needy into one's home, to share a meal and one's family life has a much greater impact than merely saying friendly words about or to them; in shared love, the child participates in a mutual exchange of love and joy.

QUESTIONS FOR THOUGHT AND DISCUSSION

1. What significance do personal experience and exploration have in a child's putting meaning to words? What implication does this have for a parent nurturing a child's faith?

2. What color would you choose to describe a particular experience like: Father's work? Mother's work? Summer vacations? Movies? Going to church?

3. What has been your experience in reading to your children? Do you have favorite reading materials or a best time?

4. How do you manage television with your child? Do you watch television with your child? How might you creatively utilize what he watches? What do you watch together? How much television does your child watch each day? Do you have rules about television use that both your child and you understand?

CHAPTER EIGHTEEN
Mine, Yours, and Ours

Love of neighbor and responsibility are difficult concepts for a five-year old. Can parents teach a child to live in solidarity with others?

He's Got the Whole World in His Hand, is an old favorite that has been sung by children all over the world. It expresses God's care for the world God created. God is alive and near and sustaining the world and its life every minute of every day.

GOD'S CO-WORKERS

The future of the world certainly lies in God's hands. But God uses people including parents and children to carry out God's purposes.

Humankind was created to be God's co-workers in this world. Men and women have been given the mission of using creation for the joy and benefit of all and are faced with the great challenge of teaching children to care for each other and the natural world around them. Through modern technology the whole world has come closer and become more interdependent. More than ever, the world is dependent on parents and children taking care of the earth and each other.

Love of neighbor and stewardship of the earth are difficult but crucial concepts young children can and must learn early.

SHARING

Neighborly love is about sharing with another. Sharing is a concrete
action that children can understand. When a chocolate bar is shared
equally between siblings, measured and cut in half with care, a sense
of fairness or justice is highly developed early among young children!

Understanding fairness doesn't mean that a child will always be willing to share. Parents have often experienced how difficult it can be
for a child to lend favorite toys to others. Conflicts between young
children most often break out because one does not want to share a
toy.

It is not easy for a child at this age to understand that others want
what she wants, that other children want to play with the same toy,
or that others need comforting as much as she does. It appears as if
the child is not able to put herself into the others' situation.
However, a parent should not underestimate children. With a little
help, they can learn to share with others early in their lives. Angie
found that when she shared some of her fruit juice with three-year-
old Mark, he, in turn, wanted to share with his eighteen-month-old
sister, Adriane.

SHARING CAN BE NOURISHED

Teaching a child to share is not primarily a question of technique or
theoretical instruction about neighborly love and solidarity. The
most important component in a child's learning to share is a warm,
loving, and caring relationship between the parent and child.

This does not mean just hugs and cuddles. Parental caring is
expressed concretely through the ways a parent regularly treats the
child—the way a parent provides for necessary material needs, time
and attention, rules and boundaries, forgiveness and comfort.

A child's experience of being loved, creates his foundation for being
able to give love. A child's love is a thank you for love.

ADULT MODELS WHO SHARE

It is well known that parents are children's most important role models. Parents can explain to children that they are to share and that sharing is important.

But, because words are transparent, it is more important that the child sees action behind the words. Does the child see a parent contributing when money is needed for a specific project? What does the child see when Dad drives past someone standing beside the road with a gasoline can in his hand? What is the parent's response to television reports from refugee camps? How does the child see a parent responding when an immigrant family moves into the neighborhood?

WHEN A CHILD DOES NOT SHARE

Every day is full of sharing-conflicts for a young child. Jonathan's friend Amy is visiting him. He is building a tower with blocks while Amy colors. Amy decides to join Jonathan in his construction work. She pulls down the tower and tries to take the blocks away from Jonathan.

This familiar situation presents a parent an opportunity to work with children concerning sharing. Both Jonathan and Amy need help in understanding what the other experiences in this play situation. A child must be helped to project his thoughts and feelings into someone else so as to see what is happening from another's perspective. A parent might well direct Jonathan's attention to Amy's desire to play with the blocks, too. At the same time a parent might explain to Amy how disappointing it is for Jonathan when his careful work has been pulled down.

Through such attention and explanation, a parent can redirect a child's self-focused energy to another by encouraging the children to project themselves into the other's feelings and wishes. The next step is to invite the two children to find and choose an option where the feelings and desires of both children can be honored. In this instance, the goal might be to have the children share the work or to take turns or to divide up the blocks, etc.

ROLE-PLAYING

When children play "Mommy-Daddy-Child," "hospital," "shop," "bus driver," and so on, they are living others' roles and professions. This playtime provides practice in shifting the child's attention to another. By playing varied roles in family and community life, children become concretely acquainted with what it's like to be someone else. A child learns something about what a bus driver does and how she and the passengers communicate with each other.

Children engage in this play on their own. Parents can expand these experiences in role-playing by bringing to the child's attention the many different roles and tasks in community life. Other such experiences through which a child can learn to empathize with another can be gained indirectly through stories, reading, television and tours.

LIFE IS A GIFT

Parents can begin early in children's lives to help them understand that everything people own has been given by God by joining together with their children in thanking God for these gifts. Through prayer both experience the graciousness of God concretely.

Christians believe that personal abilities and possessions have been given for the good of others so that God's purpose will be accomplished and the world will be a good place for all people. This can be taught best to children by making them a part of concrete actions.

The Bible is full of stories that give concrete and nourishing examples of how God cares for God's people by using persons who share with each other. A good example is the story of Jesus feeding the five thousand. The young boy in the story gives children a model with which they can identify. In this story, both children and adults demonstrate how Jesus uses what people have to offer, although it seems to be very little. Children can see that if one person is willing to share, there will be enough for all.

Humankind has received all that is needed. God has not only given the earth and everything people need to be sustained, God has also given the greatest gift of all—the gift of the Savior, Jesus Christ. Jesus came to share the humanity of both parents and children, their joys and their pain. He gave his life for their sake. God's sharing has not been half-hearted—it has been complete and perfect.

To be God's child is to receive God's gifts in thanksgiving and to share with others. The love of God's children is their thank you for God's love.

QUESTIONS FOR THOUGHT AND DISCUSSION

1. Can you talk with your child about God's graciousness using yours and your child's shared experiences? What experiences would you use?

2. How might you help your child understand the other's experience in connection with a conflict over sharing? How might a parent use situations from everyday life, from books, television programs and so forth, to teach a child other-centered awareness and empathy?

3. What might the statement, "A child's love is thank you for love they've received," mean?

4. Many families have financially supported a child in a developing country through mission organizations. Does your family do anything like this?

CHAPTER NINETEEN

Authority - Obedience - Assertiveness

"What about expecting a child to be obedient?" Can a child who is obedient ever become independent? It is not always popular and often is controversial to speak about authority in child rearing. Is there a difference between authoritative and authoritarian child rearing? Can obedience be understood as more than subservience and blind submission?

PARENTS ARE AUTHORITIES

Parents exercise authority over their children because they influence them whether the parent wants to or not. Parents can't escape providing an emotional climate and making decisions for their children. Moreover, wise exercise of this inherent authority is a part of parents' responsibility. Young children look up to their parents, imitate them, and identify with them. Children themselves see their parents as their authorities.

TWO EXTREMES

In exercising their authority there are two extremes parents must avoid. One is total abdication of authority which gives the child complete freedom to follow his impulses while the adult parent avoids interfering in the child's activity. This extreme is often called permissive parenting.

The other extreme is authoritarianism in which the parent seeks total control of the child. Such an approach often fills the child with terror. Authoritarian parenting is characterized by force, misuses of power, demand for blind obedience, and a lack of ability to listen to the child.

Constructive parenting exercises authentic authority, which is built on confidence and genuine respect rather than fear. Authoritative parents know children's needs for boundaries and direction. The goal of authoritative parenting is a child with an inner compass of life-giving values who is becoming an independent and responsible person.

Parental authority and guidance can provide reasonable expectations of obedience that provide the moral foundation for an independent child. Children do not become independent by following their own impulses and whims. Children do not become independent cowering under a severe dictator. On the contrary, from the very beginning of a child's life the way to independence and interdependence leads through early dependence, parental love and guidance, and good boundaries and norms set by good caregivers.

OBEDIENCE WITH UNDERSTANDING

Obedience can take many forms. Blind obedience as subservience undercuts a child's journey toward independence. In blind obedience the demand for obedience is not explained or justified. "You shall...because I say so!"

When obedience teaches children that rules and norms are for their good and the good of others, it is constructive and fosters both independence and interdependence in children. Obedience with explanation and purpose fosters meaning and thoughtfulness in the child.

To the best of their abilities, authoritative parents explain to their children the rules and norms they want them to follow.

If children are to be independent and responsible people, they must internalize or make these norms and values their own. This process begins as children first learn obedience to their parents and the regulations and norms their parents clearly state and explain to them. Gradually a child struggles, pushing and testing these norms until she makes them her own. In the process, parental authority brings forth inner authority and an independent conscience develops. To be independent is to be obedient toward one's own conscience.

PRAISE AND PUNISHMENT

Authority and obedience raise the question of the roles of praise and punishment in child rearing. When parents practice genuine authority with independence and responsibility as the goal, they will seek to influence their child with encouragement and praise. Both research and experience demonstrate that encouragement and praise are more influential than punishment. Praise and encouragement emphasize what is good and just both in the child and the child's behavior, while punishment focuses only on that which is wrong.

If punishment is to be used in the discipline of a child, the punishment must be focused and teach a specific lesson. The clear purpose of punishment must be teaching the child to differentiate between right and wrong. The goal is developing the child's inner control mechanism, sense of responsibility, and accountability.

Even though they may be done with the best of intentions, not all methods of punishment can be justified. Methods that unnecessarily humiliate a child or destroy a child's worth as a person, have no place in bringing up a child.

MISUSING PHYSICAL AND PSYCHOLOGICAL POWER

The use of corporal punishment is the most confusing and controversial among parents and child-rearing experts. There are major differences between a strong parental hand which takes a firm and secure grip of a child, and the powerful hand that slaps or a fist that beats. There is also a real difference between a less spontaneous tap on a child's bottom or shoulder to emphasize the seriousness of a "no" and a beating. For followers of Jesus Christ such treatment of a child is out of the question.

There are also forms of psychological torture, such as when a parent confronts a child with such threats as: "If you are not good, Mom and Dad won't love you any more." Sarcasm, jeers, taunting, and so forth, result only in breaking down a child's self-respect and can be more destructive than physical violence.

IF PARENTS MUST PUNISH

The following principles are good to have in mind if a parent punishes a child:

- There must be a logical connection between the deed and the punishment;

- The punishment must be reasonable and just;

- The punishment should come immediately after the deed; and,

- It is important to be clear with the child as to why he is being punished.

Suppose Jonathan creates a disturbance during a family gathering and in spite of repeated warnings, continues to disrupt conversation. In so doing he makes himself obnoxious to all present. A logical punishment might, for example, be to send him to his room to think about what he was done, to stay there until he has decided to change his behavior. To remove a favorite privilege is also a punishment most children can understand.

THE BIBLE AS AUTHORITY

When the Bible states that children should obey their parents, it is not primarily out of consideration for parents. Neither does it mean that parents do not make mistakes. Through obeying one's parent, a child's conscience can be shaped by God's message and will.

This divine shaping of conscience progresses more surely if the child's parents' wills are subject to God's will as revealed in God's Word. The Bible states clearly the foundation of authoritative parenting: "Parents, never drive your children to resentment but in bringing them up, correct them and guide them as the Lord does." (Ephesians 6:4)

In the development of such a conscience, it is important to teach a child to rightly use the Bible. Parents can be a child's major Bible teacher by regularly reading the Bible to and with their child, and taking God's Word seriously in their own lives. As parents read and live God's Word, the child learns that the Bible is not only a book of ancient history, but that God through the Scriptures communicates to them day by day.

GUIDING A CHILD TOWARD INDEPENDENCE
Parenting grounded in God's message and will provides a sold basis for a child's independence. The ultimate goal of a parent is not subjecting a child to a parent's or another's authority, but that the child comes to know and obey God, her maker, redeemer, and comforter.

Ultimately, a child is to be raised to become free and considerate in relation to all human authority. Such independence means that the child herself will answer for her own life before her Savior and Lord.

Such a perspective is liberating for parents. Parents have no guarantee nor can parents finally control how a child will respond to their best efforts. Parents' task is to take a child by the hand and gently but firmly walk together with the child the way God has taught them to walk. Parents can do no more. When the day of parental leadership ends, the child has responsibility for choosing her own way.

QUESTIONS FOR THOUGHT AND DISCUSSION
1. Can you find examples from your own experience, history, and literature of both permissive and authoritarian parenting? How do each of these differ from authoritative parenting?

2. Some parents argue that guiding a child toward independence is guiding a child toward disobedience. What do you think?

3. Children can easily discern a parent's vulnerability and exploit them in order to get their own way. These parental points of vulnerability often are feelings of guilt, sense of responsibility, unfortunate habits, self-occupation, reputation as parents, etc.

   Eric begs for candy at the store despite the fact that he had agreed earlier with this mother that they would not buy any that day. His mother says "no," and Eric argues loudly with her and calls her stingy and mean. "You never buy anything for me!"

   Consider three different responses on the part of his mother:

   A) She submits: "Okay, it's been a while, you can have it."

   B) She argues: "Forgoing the candy is for your best; it isn't long since you had candy."

   C) She leads: "It's a pity you have such a mean mom!"

   Did anyone win in these three responses? How can a parent avoid having her child draw her into such a battle for power? How would you handle this situation?

4. How do you see punishment fitting into bringing up your child? Think of punishment you could use in your child's pre-school age.

CHAPTER TWENTY
Celebrations and Traditions

"Jingle bells, jingle bells..." Christmas is connected with the joy of children. Most parents have many happy memories from their own childhood Christmases. These memories are usually tied to traditions that parents want to preserve and hand down to their children. On the other hand, some parents have few memories of Christmas that are positive and wish to create their own, constructive Christmas traditions.

Children love routines and rituals. They enjoy doing fun activities together the same way they've been done before. Thus children become fond of traditions that are repeated from day to day, week to week, and year to year. Traditions provide roots, identity, and values.

FAMILY TRADTIONS

Traditions bind a family together and create a sense of belonging as well as identity. Because of the fast pace of contemporary life and its massive changes, many families have not only lost their traditions but also a sense of their meaning and worth. "Its only tradition!" parents often say, and dismiss powerful vehicles for passing values on to children. Certainly parents should not carry on traditions uncritically. Lost, meaningless, or restrictive traditions should be replaced with new and better ones.

Christmas is a premier time of traditions. Christmas demonstrates the value of traditions both for children and the family as an unit. At Christmas, mother and father often bring together their own childhood traditions. These are blended with new family traditions in which children can find roots, identity, and values.

OPEN FAMILIES

Many families celebrate Christmas with grandparents, other relatives, and friends. A family also may expand its circle by inviting a lonely person or a refugee family to celebrate Christmas with the family. Adding shared-family Christmas preparations and traditions, as well as congregational and community gatherings, into their tradition bonds families with each other, the church, and the community.

ENRICHING THE CHILD'S CHRISTMAS JOURNEY

Christmas is a festival for children not only because of the many family traditions. More than any other time of the church year, Christmas presents the Gospel's message to children. The Christmas story found in Luke's Gospel is a story that engages children. The story of Mary and Joseph and the babe lying in a manger in a place with cows and sheep is concrete and living. It is easy for children to create mental pictures of what happened in Bethlehem. Through Christmas celebration song, gifts, and decorations the Christmas message becomes concrete and alive.

Many of our familiar Christmas carols center on words of peace and joy. For example, in "Hark the Herald Angels Sing," we hear the words "Peace on earth, and Mercy mild." "Joy to the World" is probably the most familiar Christmas carol that speaks of joy. Christmas peace and joy are built on the wonder that the holy and omnipotent God became human and lived here on earth.

This mystery often causes more problems for adults than for children. Many children can understand the message of Christmas more easily than adults. At Christmas even adults are like children again, full of child-like wonder for a mystery that cannot be grasped intellectually, but by faith.

ADVENT PREPARATIONS

Christmas preparations during the season of Advent are as important as the day itself. For children preparation creates a feeling of expectancy and excitement. If unrealistic expectations are created for children, Christmas can be a disappointment. Too much stress and bother will not leave much energy for the memory and celebration of the event itself. What will children understand of the deepest meanings of Christmas, if preparation centers only on shopping, gifts, and food? For this reason, it is important for parents to focus their preparations, centering them on the coming of the Christ child.

Advent means arrival. Parents can fill advent weeks with conversation and ritual pointing toward the arrival of the One whose birth we will celebrate on Christmas. Developing traditions that symbolize and emphasize Christmas' central content helps children understand what to expect. In the context of the greatest birth and life of all history, baking, house cleaning, shopping, sending cards, decorating, etc. will have new meaning.

CHILDREN CAN PREPARE FOR CHRISTMAS

Children can be encouraged to participate in Advent activities that prepare the way to Christmas. Baking and decorating, as well as sending cards and giving gifts all stimulate a child's creative abilities. In addition, these activities foster family togetherness and provide common, meaningful projects that both parents and child can enjoy. Churches can expand parent-child projects by arranging intergenerational Advent festivals and workshops.

Utilizing an Advent calendar is a popular activity in many families. Marking each day with a surprise, caring conversation and singing Advent and Christmas songs can become a mini-ritual or tradition in the family. A spirit of celebration and anticipation can accompany the lighting of Advent candles each Sunday. Using simple instruments, a tape, or CD, parents and children can learn new songs on each of the Advent Sundays and then sing them each day of the coming week.

Songs are vital in Christian Christmas traditions and in nurturing the faith of a young child. Christmas songs and hymns are cultural as well as religious treasures that tell the story of the Christian message in direct and simple ways. Children are poorer if they never learn these and other songs of the faith.

CHRISTMAS TRADITIONS

A great variety of traditions have grown up around the world during the past centuries. In some countries, it's waking on Christmas morning to celebrate with one's closest family members. For many children, gathering with other family members at the family Christmas tree is the high point of celebrating Christmas. Some families include singing of Christmas carols; others may share stories and open gifts. In some countries tradition may include moving to the church or out into the community where the family joins others, holding hands and walking around the Christmas tree while singing Christmas songs.

Many families celebrate a Christmas dinner on either Christmas Eve or Christmas Day. The meal becomes a time for reading the Christmas story from the Bible, singing a favorite Christmas song, and telling Christmas stories from times past.

Christmas celebrates God's giving God's son Jesus, who came to share all he had with us. Sharing gifts is a natural expression of marking this gift of God through giving and sharing with others. Many families choose with their children, needy or lonely persons of differing ages for whom to make gifts. These people often are invited to Christmas dinner and included in the family's traditions of celebration.

Nothing is more fitting than attending worship at a congregation during Christmas holidays. During these worship services, parents can take the lead in developing exciting family Christmas worship services as one of the options for Christmas Eve or Christmas Day. Even though the story telling, drama, puppets, prayers, music, and songs in these services can be chosen particularly for children, they are intergenerational favorites enjoyed by parents and grandparents as well.

Parents need not be afraid that children are too young to understand Christmas traditions. It is important to begin as early as possible establishing a family's customs and traditions in celebrating faith at Christmas. As children grow, they will have the opportunity to gradually discover the meaning of traditions and can be encouraged to add their own contributions to the family's roots, identity and values.

GROUP PROJECT

Rather than providing questions on theoretical and practical aspects of parenting for your consideration at the end of this chapter an idea is presented for your celebration of Christmas with your children.

SANTA'S WORKSHOP

Children and adults might gather as a group to make Christmas decorations, a manager scene, Christmas gifts; bake traditional foods; learn carols; practice a pageant; etc. One or many families might do this together; other families from church or the neighborhood might be invited.

During the workshop, gifts could be made for people in need, one of whom each of the families might adopt and care for and with during the coming year.

CHAPTER TWENTY ONE

Children and Public Worship

"Are worship services for young children?"

"Children understand very little of what is occurring."

"Worship services are boring for a child this age."

"It is so difficult to get them to be quiet!"

Most parents any Sunday Morning

ARE CHILDREN MATURE ENOUGH FOR PUBLIC WORSHIP?

A child's capacity for public worship is often underestimated. Children understand more than most adults presume. It is not important that a child understand every word spoken in the worship service. Children are significantly engaged by seeing and experiencing. They are immersed in music and song. They see the sanctuary, banners, vestments, the altar and its paraments. They see processions of children and adults in robes. They see puppets that tell

God's story. They see pastors and parents who kneel and pray, who read scriptures, preach, and lift their hands in blessing. Children feel the atmosphere. As they become familiar with worship and grow, they learn to sing and participate in the liturgy, pray the Lord's Prayer, and repeat the confession of faith.

Children will learn these activities of worship more quickly if they have parents or another adult worship sitter who will bring them to worship and coach them through each aspect of worship. If there are more children in a family than there are parents or adults, develop a relationship with a surrogate family member who can help during worship. Parents or worship sitters can explain to children what is happening in the service, as well as tell them of the significance of the symbols in the sanctuary.

As a child grows older, the more complex activities of the worship service with their symbolic meanings can be explained and assimilated. Parents can explain that when the pastor turns toward the altar, it is because the pastor is speaking to God, that the colors used are changed according to the church calendar, and that the congregation rises to its feet out of respect to hear the pastor read the Gospel.

HOLY, AWESOME, AND FULL OF WONDER

There is much in worship for children to discover that engenders curiosity and wonder. God is holy—awesome—that which is different - an occasion for children's exploration and imagination. In these matters, children are often more open than adults. Children's curiosity and wonder can be their first step toward understanding.

Even parents will never be able to understand everything in the church or the faith. It is important for children, as well as parents, to retain a child-like wonder when meeting that which is holy. Perhaps children can be their parents' teachers regarding this important aspect of faith.

DESIGNING WORSHIP FOR CHILDREN ALSO

Children belong in public worship. Jesus left no doubt: "Let the little children come unto me and forbid them not. For of such is the Kingdom of God—Whoever does not humble himself as a little child, shall not enter the Kingdom of God" Children are, in Jesus' words, never too young to come to him, meet him, respond to him, worship him. Their capacities for trust and awe are present from their earliest beginnings. Parents carry children to the font when they are received in baptism; parents can safely bring them with them to worship services in the years that follow.

PARENTAL WORSHIP AND PRAYER

When it comes to worship and prayer, as in so many other areas of parenting, children learn more through what parents do than what they say. When parents attend worship or Bible study regularly or spend personal time in prayer, they teach their children that engaging and glorifying God are important for grown ups. If parents fail to participate in such activities of the faith, children are either never introduced to faith or learn that for the most important people in their lives the practice of faith is unimportant.

The best way to teach a child the forms and content of the worship service is for parents to participate actively in the liturgy. A 70-year old says, "I was only seven years old when my father died, but even now I have the image of my father folding his hands, praying, responding, singing, rising, and listening to the pastor. He demonstrated the worship service for me, and that meant far more than the words I heard and barely understood."

WAITING UNTIL THE CHILD WANTS TO PARTICIPATE?

A child's desire for worship usually doesn't materialize on its own. If a child is going to be interested in a football game and perhaps even play football, the child must have an opportunity to experience football, to learn the rules and participate in learning the game. Basically, children learn about worship in the same way. The desire and interest to participate must be awakened and developed through involvement. Because worship is far more important than football or other sports and activities, parents must see to it that children have the opportunity to become acquainted with worship services from their earliest years.

LEADING CHILDREN INTO WORSHIP

Forcing a child into faith is neither advisable nor possible. If children are to be interested in worship, it is primarily a question of a significant person in the family laying the foundation.

An important step in laying this foundation is setting a routine for family life on Sundays. It is important, in as much as it is possible, for families to make Sundays different than other days – perhaps even a family day to which the children can look forward with anticipation and pleasure. One might begin the day with a leisurely time for breakfast when everyone is together and has occasion to be engaged in common conversation and play. Stress and fuss in getting off to church can easily create frustration and conflict. Parents might want to plan a lunch or trip with one or more families following worship.

Planning such family times in fast-paced, twenty-first century lifestyle is difficult and requires considerable sacrifice and intentionality. However, parents who develop rhythms of family time, not only enhance their own and their child's relationship with God, but strengthen their family's solidarity and values as well.

NOISY CHILDREN IN CHURCH

Children differ from one another in their church conduct just as in other aspects of their lives. Some are still and quiet. Others can be restless and active, having difficulty keeping still. In like manner, worshipping adults differ from one another in the way they respond to other people's children. When accusing glances from a neighboring pew become more frequent and intense, a parent can lose courage in bringing his child next Sunday.

Active children have as much a place in worship as adults. A bit of restlessness and a few sounds should be tolerated, even as children must learn to be considerate. A picture book, some paper and crayons, and soft toys are helpful for those who need to release their energy while sitting in the pew. Sometimes parents take off their children's shoes so they make little, if any, noise when they wander up and down in front of a pew. When a child begins to scream, there is no cause to be embarrassed by leaving with the child for a calming walk outside.

CHILD-FRIENDLY WORSHIP AND CHURCHES

Children belong in public worship. Therefore, worship services and general church activities should be geared for children as well as adults. There are many ways of making this a reality throughout the congregation.

Intergenerational, family worship services are especially well suited to children. Children can take part in worship services through singing their music, processions, short plays, etc. Children's ministry leaders can develop projects that directly relate to the scripture for the day and can be worked on during the sermon.

Puppets, clowns, story telling, the regular appearance of Bible characters during worship are especially engaging events for children. Parents should not be afraid to suggest that these activities for their children be included in worship. Whatever is done to make worship child-friendly, need not take from either children or adults those experiences which challenge them to grow.

CHILDREN AND COMMUNION

In most churches today, children either commune or are encouraged to come with their parents to Holy Communion. Some parents are in doubt about what they should do, and practices vary from church to church. Some congregations encourage parents to take children along to communion so that the pastor can lay hands on their heads and bless them. Other congregations commune all baptized children. This practice includes children with their families in the church's worship life. As children experience communion in this way, they become acquainted with the elements and activities of communion, and their natural curiosity will encourage them to ask questions about its meaning. In answering their questions, parents have an excellent teaching opportunity that make it possible for both parents and children to participate more fully in the sacrament and at the same time learn more of its significance.

Although no one ever completely understands all that happens in Holy Communion, both children and adults can receive its gifts of grace. In Holy Communion grace is so concrete and immediate it can be tasted.

WORSHIP IN THE HOME

Reading from the Bible, praying, and singing together at home are also forms of worship. In these activities, parents can use prayers and hymns from a great variety of sources including children's songbooks and the scripture texts for the coming week. Private worship at home and public worship at church can inform and support each other when planned and coordinated imaginatively.

Because life is hectic, it's not always easy to work out times of family worship. However, even in the busiest families, bedtimes, meal times, driving in the car, sick days, baptismal anniversaries, family outings, and vacations provide opportune occasions for private, family worship. The church year with its festivals provides one framework for these devotions in the home.

LENT AND EASTER

Of the three great festivals in the church year, Christmas is undoubtedly the most celebrated both in congregations and at home. Equally important in the church are the celebrations of Easter and Pentecost.

Easter is the Church's most important festival. As with Christmas, Easter also has its time of preparation, known as Lent. During Lent, fasting can be an experience of sacrifice and the imitation of Christ.

To fast is to abstain from eating certain foods as a way of disciplining oneself in following Jesus' word and example. The Christian community, during earlier times, fasted 40 days during Lent in remembrance of Jesus' fast in the desert.

Sacrifices such as fasting are often foreign to secular people in prosperous and indulgent societies. Because many families live with the stress and conscience-numbing pressures of materialism, including a sacrificial experience during the season of Lent can provide new perspectives on the needs of others. These sacrifices could take the form of eliminating desserts and candy or merely eating simpler food. Families might make this experience even more meaningful by contributing the money saved by making these sacrifices to their church's mission program, emergency food fund, or other programs the church has to help people in need.

During the final week of Lent and this period of fasting, a family might follow Christ from Palm Sunday to Easter by reading the events of his journey during that week as recorded in Scripture. While it is difficult to explain Good Friday's dramatic events to small children, simply letting the Scriptures speak for themselves, children will come to know that Jesus was crucified, died and rose again, and is living today.

The message of Easter is rich in pictures that are excellent starting points for activities with children. A family or several families in a congregation might construct a landscape with a grave in a cave much like one might do with a manger scene at Christmas. Colored eggs, chickens, and bunnies are traditions that remind children that Easter represents the new life Jesus won for us through his death and resurrection.

QUESTIONS FOR THOUGHT AND DISCUSSION

1. What were your childhood experiences with church attendance, Sunday school, Bible reading, and prayer at home that had special meaning for you and may inform faith practices in your home now?

2. What place does reading the Bible, prayers, and singing the songs of faith have in your home? What among the many options of family devotions, evening prayers, singing, and reading the Scriptures, faith in daily life conversation, family mission projects, etc. are most effective in your family?

3. When a four-, five-, or six-year-old child resists church attendance because "it's so boring," how would you respond?

4. Are children invited to Holy Communion in your congregation? Are they encouraged to commune, receive a blessing, or both?

CHAPTER TWENTY-TWO

Dealing With Loss and Death

When death strikes, children should be encouraged to participate in the grief. In a situation where parents feel overwhelmed in their sorrow, it is easy for them to forget children or believe children are too fragile to deal with death. It is best during times of loss for children to be at the very heart of grieving.

"Does it hurt to die?" "Do only old people die?" "Why are dead people buried?" "How can they get from the ground to heaven?" "Do dead people lie with their eyes open?" "Do they get dirt in their eyes?" "Can people play in heaven?"

Sooner or later, children will raise questions concerning death, burial, and heaven. A child's experiences of these times of loss and grief will greatly influence the kind of questions children will ask. For some children the questions can be personal and full of emotion, especially in connection to a death in the family, or the death of a favorite pet. Other children ask questions out of curiosity in attempts to make sense out of their experiences of loss, because children at these early ages hear about war, accidents, suffering, and death—especially through television.

CHILDREN'S UNDERSTANDINGS OF DEATH

A child's understanding of death at age three or four is usually unrealistic and is understood as a long or short time-out or recess after which the dead person will live again. One can see this during play, when children will play dead. "Bang, bang, you're dead!" And the dead one falls to the ground and rolls around, lies still, then is suddenly up and playing again.

Children often do not understand that death is irrevocable. After grandfather dies, the child might ask: "How long will he be dead? Will he be hungry in the grave? Is he cold down there?" Even so children can suffer confusion, sorrow, and bereavement when someone close to them dies. It is typical of this age that such emotions shift often and are short lived.

Gradually children learn that death means an end to life. At this point, they begin asking the deeper and more difficult questions of what it is like to be dead, why a person must die, and where one goes after death.

PROVIDING CHILDREN FACTUAL INFORMATION ABOUT DEATH

Even though explaining death to a child is difficult, her questions and curiosity must be taken seriously. It can be tempting for parents to treat death lightly by saying that "it is only sleep" or that grandfather "is only on a trip." Such expressions can easily give children wrong impressions and false expectations. Even saying, "Grandma has gone to heaven to be with Jesus," can cause problems. Young Carrie couldn't understand why they couldn't take an airplane to go see Grandma. If heaven and Jesus are so far away that we can't visit, she wasn't sure she would ever want to go that far away.

There is no reason to hold back on whatever knowledge a parent has about death. It helps to be concrete: Death means that the person can no longer breathe, that the dead can no longer hear, see, speak, or feel and will not return. This is not easy to understand—either for children or for adults, which is all the more reason for children to be included so that both children and adults can wonder together over the mysteries of death.

BE OPEN AND TRUTHFUL

Pre-school children are more afraid that their parents will die than that death will strike them. A six-year-old will sometimes worry about what he will do if his parents die. "Who am I going to hug if you die, Daddy?" His concerns can be so great that the child will cry himself to sleep worrying about his parents' dying. A good conversation about who will take care of him if one of his parents dies, can often be more calming than to reassure that it will be a long, long time until a parent dies.

It is vitally important that parents tell the truth about death. Many parents want to protect their children against everything that concerns death. But protecting children from death is shortsighted and can become deceptive. A mother wanting to spare her son undue concern had not told him that his father was about to die; rather, she said that he would soon return home. When the father died, the boy realized that his mother had lied to him, which weakened his confidence in his mother and made it difficult for him to trust her word.

CHILDREN, DYING AND FUNERALS

When death strikes, children must be encouraged to share in the sorrow. In a situation where parents feel overwhelmed in their sorrow, it is easy for them to forget children or believe children are too fragile to deal with death and keep them away from saying goodbye at the funeral. It is best during times of loss for children to be at the heart of the grieving. As far as possible child should be with those they are closest to in their family. It is good for them to be present as family and friends cry together and talk about the one who died.

Ordinarily children should attend the funeral of a loved one. If they strongly protest, they should be allowed to stay home with someone they know and trust. Funerals confirm that the dead person is truly dead and help children overcome their denial. Through participation in the service children receive data that helps avoid frightening fantasies about funerals. Funerals are farewell ceremonies that help children handle their grief.

Parents can do significant work in preparing children for funerals. They can explain the order of the service, how it will move from the church or chapel to the burial at the cemetery. They can explain that the coffin will be placed in the church before the service begins and that the pastor will read words from the Bible to give hope and comfort. They can continue by describing how the coffin will be carried out and let down into a grave in the cemetery or placed in a furnace to become ashes, which will later be placed in the earth. It may even be of help, both for the children and adults, to sing at least one of the hymns of the service before the funeral itself. During the funeral service, the children need familiar adults, preferably family members around them. After the funeral, children should have help working through his impressions by drawing pictures and talking about their experience.

SORROW IS WORKED OUT

Children's sorrow can be deeply felt, even if they do not cry. Children do not always express their sorrow in the same way as adults do. Children should have the freedom to express their sorrow in their own way, whether it be sobbing or serious thought and conversation.

Children's state of mind can change quickly even in connection with sorrow. Parents should not be shocked or hurt if immediately following a funeral, children begin to play casually and joyfully. Children must not be pressured to think about death all the time—something they are unable to do. Play is one of the ways children work through their sorrow.

THE DIFFICULT "WHY?"

The many why-questions become immensely difficult when death strikes suddenly and unexpectedly, as when another...especially a friend...is killed in a traffic accident. Children experience such a death as painful, unjust and meaningless; all explanations will seem to fall flat.

In such cases it is easy for both children and adults to blame God. "Why did God let the car run over her? Why didn't God stop the car?" Both children and adults can become bitter toward God, and ask, "Can one trust a God who lets such things happen?"

At such times it is well for parents to admit to children that they do not understand. At the same time, a parent can tell children that God does not wish bad things to happen. As carefully as possible, a parent should tell children that God is good and is not responsible for that which is evil and bad. Above all, parents should let their children experience the omnipresence of a God who is close to those who suffer. Instead of accusing God and giving God the blame for that which is bad, a parent can take children to God in prayer using either their own words or one of the Psalms to pour out their bitter feelings complaints and doubts.

"WHERE DO WE GO WHEN WE DIE, MOMMY?"

Children are curious about what will happen after death. The question of life after death is crucial, especially for Christians who believe in the resurrection of the dead. The Bible uses many different images and expressions that complement each other, thus providing bits and pieces of a reality which neither children nor adults will totally understand. The Bible writes about heaven as a place where God is. It announces that Jesus has gone before to prepare this place. The Bible speaks of heaven coming to God's people as some day when God will make all things new—a time when everything will be as it was meant to be—a time very different from anything that can be imagined.

Parents and children are bound by their limited impressions and knowledge as they talk about this new life in heaven with God. For children, the images are usually concrete. A parent will see this when a child comes with her many and unique questions on how it is in heaven, how one gets there, etc. A parent ought not dismiss these questions or shrug off these concrete images as necessarily wrong. A child's concrete ideas can be as close to expressing these eternal truths as an adult's more abstract propositions. What is decisive is that children (and adults!) have assurance that God will keep Jesus Christ's promise that God's people will rise to new life with God.

It is important that the images used in the Bible express that heaven is a life spent with God, a life that Jesus has prepared and therefore can only be good. As an example, when a six-year-old asks if there will be toys in heaven, what is he actually asking? There are good reasons to believe that he is concerned about being happy in heaven; in other words—is it good to be with God? And it will be! A parent can allow a child's imagination to soar. Nothing is too amazing when describing how good life will be with God. At the same time, a parent must help a child understand that human impressions and imagination will never measure up to the actual wonder of this life with God.

FUTURE HOPE

It is not unusual for children to believe that they will have to be good in order to go to heaven. If this is the case, parents have an opportunity to help them understand that heaven is a gift from God for those who believe in Jesus.

In a world filled with anxiety, suffering, and death, it is wonderful for a parent to be able to point a child toward the One who cares for her and will never leave or forsake the parent or child. This assurance of living in the proximity of Jesus and in God's care, gives both children and adults a feeling of security and hope for the future. "In both life and death, I know my way, and in both life and death, I am confident."

QUESTIONS FOR THOUGHT AND DISCUSSION

1. Some parents wish to shield children from suffering and death. What might the basis for their thinking? Might this attitude do injustice to a child? How?

2. "Grandfather is only asleep" or "Grandmother has gone on a trip." Would you use these words to describe an elder's death to your child? If not, how would you do so?

3. Have your children ever attended a funeral with you? How did they respond? How did or might you prepare them? What did or might you do with them after the funeral service?

4. A five-year old asks his parents: "Will all children go to heaven?" How would you answer this question with your child?

5. Many children experience anxiety about the future and can even ask such questions as, "Will I live to be as old as you, Dad or Mom?" What can parents do to give their children hope for the future and courage for going on with their lives in the face of loss?

IN CONCLUSION...
AND ON TO THE NEXT

When a family is created by birth or adoption, each parent has dreams - for the child, for the relationship, for gifts developed, for experiences shared, for memories to cherish, for the love that flows from God to parent to child and back again. There are fears, too. What if I'm not a good enough parent? What if this child isn't the one I've always dreamed of? What if she doesn't like me? What if I don't understand him? Will I be patient enough? Do I have the insight to know what he needs? Will I say "no" at the right times for the right reasons? Will I bring her up to be all that God created her to be? Do I know how to nurture faith and life in this little one?

So begins the odyssey of parenting with purpose. Together we have explored the developmental ages and stages and tasks of children as they grow from birth to age six. Infants attach to their parents and primary caregivers, learning that the world is a safe place because their adults are trustworthy. Adults invest great time and attention in caring for the infant. Needs are met reliably and with great love. Infants need to experience attachment to adults in order to feel secure and learn to trust. Closeness allows the infant to endure distance and absence, trusting the loved adults to return. Enveloped in their parent's love, infants are prepared for relationship with a God of love.

Only when they feel secure can toddlers begin to explore their world, believing that age appropriate boundaries, reliably enforced by adults who love them, will keep them safe. They also delight in growing self-awareness and in exploring who they are, how others react to them, and what they can do. Their minds, too, engage in this adventure of discovery, utilizing observation, exploration and questions, questions and more questions. Adults provide answers and explanations, understanding and insights in what they say and in what they do. And those adults are a safe harbor to which children can return for comfort, reassurance and love. In this relationship, toddlers are open to understanding God as a loving parent.

Young children live in an ever enlarging world. Boundaries are expanding. Competency multiplies. Understanding grows by leaps and bounds. Reliable, loving, present adults help young children to internalize security, which is necessary to develop the courage to venture out into an expanding world. Their world of relationships also enlarges with more loved and trusted adults and childhood friends. Children begin to internalize their values and judgments, developing a conscience. Children learn to accept responsibility for their behavior ... and misbehavior. They cannot always control their impulses or predict the consequences of their expansive exploration or exuberant self-expression. They begin to experience remorse, to apologize, to crave forgiveness. Relationships need to be repaired and restored. Their image of God expands from a loving parent to the one who forgives and always, always welcomes the child back with great love and celebration. Rituals, traditions and worship open the young child to an ever expanding experience of God. God is present. God is immediate. God is with them in the painful losses and the joyous gifts. God, too, is mystery and majesty. For the young child parented with purpose, faith in God flourishes.

What comes next? In families, parents and children both grow and become more of what God created them to be. This is the odyssey of the ever unfolding, lifelong adventure of nurturing faith and life in children as we parent with purpose.